Images of the Mystic Truth

Library of Congress Catalog Card Number: 81-82432

ISBN 0-917398-10-6

Compiled and Edited by
Sal St. John Buttaci & Susan Linda Gerstle

Published by
New Worlds Unlimited, Saddle Brook, New Jersey 07662

Printed in the United States of America

FOR
poets who seek new worlds
of imagination,
each poem a steppingstone
on that road to
Truth.

INDEX

OF

AUTHORS

Margaret Giles			78
Rachel Givan		61	73
Joe Gleason Jr.			31
Emilie Glen			79
Kent Glenzer			25
Leonard Gorenstein			98
Frances Lucille Gorman			63
Shirley Anne Gorman		109	117
E.P. Govea		108	130
Virgil Graber			40
Rachel L. Grant			77
Ruthie Grant			73
Godfrey Green			96
Cynthia S. Greene			81
Heide U. Greenwald			95
Laurette Houle Gutierrez		*10	71
Carol Hamilton		112	126
Lillian Hammer			51
Pat Hancock			54
Judith E. Hannan		*7	105
Sharon L. Harris			43
Elizabeth Hartman		61	99
Velda A. Hatch			105
Diane Heald			106
Paul M. Hedeen			106
Cyndi Hellstrom		61	66
Cheryl L. Henderson			*8
Cheryl Hendry			74
Christina Heraty			100
Virginia Hilton	88	95	105
Cynthia Hines			*11
Shirley Ann Hipp			14
barb e. hobbs		94	131
jhan hochman			88
Deborah Hochstettler			35
Mark J. Hollister			129
E. Leon Hostetler		61	102
Karen L. Hotchkiss		79	92
Judith Hougen		60	114
Libby Hubbard			25
TinaMarie Hubbard			51
Carolyn J. Fairweather Hughes			90
June Lee Humphrey			33
Linda Bleser Hunt			106
Virginia L. Hunt		36	129
Barbara Hurd			28
Linda Hutton			71
Florence F. Ickes			89
Susan Ideker		82	96
Katrin Imani		78	129
Randall Jacobs			116
Nathalie Frances Jahnes			65
Gary Jedinak			33
Genevieve Johnson		68	128
Henry Johnson			121
Georgia Johnston			91
Jacqueline A. Jones		63	128
D.H. Joyner		38	75
Morris Kalmus		61	101
Joseph D. Kantor		99	111
Sita Kapadia	*10	71	113
Denise Katz		110	125
Pat Keenan		44	46
Joan L. Kelly		86	108
Nancy P. Kenny		41	124
Kathy Keogh			26
John L. Kirkhoff			87
Barbara Klapperich		13	74
Dorothy E. Kloss			70
George Knepper			128
Turia L. Knez			76
Philip J. Kokinis			22
Rose Krevit			93
Erich Krueger		23	99

Mary Jane Kuzontkoski	105	130
Diana Kwiatkowski		16
Elsie Halsey Lacy	117	124
Bruce Lader		87
Ruth Laine		19
Alana Lally		16
Bruce Langbein	112	127
Mary Frances Langford		29
Paul P. Langley		34
Rae Lannon		115
Pamela L. Laskin		43
David E. LeCount	46	94
Brenda Ledbetter		27
Judy Lee		129
Gary Lemco		99
Lori Lewis		22
Gregory Liffick	15	20
Jo Starrett Lindsey	17	95
Katherine Lithgow		32
Marta Livesay		84
A.J. Llewellyn		129
Paul L. Long	85	112
Donna Lovett		124
Jennifer Luckhardt	38	52
Claire M. Lynch		90
Aline Musyl Marks	55	86
Randall Marquardt		36
Katherine Marsh		80
Isabel Marshall	23	120
Debra Martinez		36
John Mascazine		92
Susan Masinick		112
Bertha Mayes		16
Paul K. McAfee		21
Jane McConnell	38	69
Olivia McCormack		127
Judith Anne McCrary		110

Ida M. Lister McLaughlin			24
Patricia McManus		53	127
Mark McNease			*9
Roberta Mendel		37	84
Betty D. Mercer			91
David Michaelson			109
Cheryl Micucci		86	110
Barbara Milazzo			42
Deborah S. Millman			119
Marvin Minkler		69	128
David Monreal		95	123
Kent Monroe Jr.			126
Farzana Moon			118
Beverly Moore			78
Debra Moore		78	120
Lynn Moore		30	66
Pat Mora		18	95
Jennifer Morris			60
Dianne J. Morrissey			108
Kathy Morrone		19	41
Vicki S. Mossman			130
John Mueller			22
bob mullin			48
Carolyn Murphy		105	107
Thelma Murphy	88	122	126
Betty Muschar			47
Alicia J. Muse			93
Ellen H. Muse		99	131
Dawn Myers			15
Natalie A. Nalepinski			37
Alan Napier			60
LaMoyne Nations			102
Wayne Nelson		29	80
Nicholas		89	115
Robert J. Oberg			14
Julian Ocean			40
Valerie J. Olson		13	20

Richard T. Orlando	62	100
Maureen O'Toole	50	107
Eleanor Otto		100
Sherry Owens-Austin		76
Joseph M. Pallozzi	30	69
David J. Patarozzi		114
Barbara Pearson	20	96
Janet Pembor		14
Dollyna K. Perry		49
Albert Pertha	67	96
Martha Peterson	41	87
Martina A. Philipp	64	82
Lois Taft Phoebus		118
Kari Piske		83
Caroly Poe		15
Shilo Prentice		48
Robert Preswick		63
William Price		109
Alexandra S. Prober		33
Gloria H. Procsal	21	57
Jill Purvis		35
Garnet Quiett	85	116
Joyce Randolph	26	121
Gail Razinsky		23
Floyd M. Regan Jr.	27	121
Patricia Rexrode	51	97
Eugene Rich		36
Jeff Richardson	89	102
Kevin Richert		126
Bonnie Riechert	102	125
Cynthia C. Ripp	124	126
Peter Ritchie, Jr.	46	99
Bev Fox Roberson	49	131
Matthew Rogers		42
Steven B. Rogers	90	130
Rebecca S. Rossignol *8	68	94
Alexis Rotella	56	68

Rose Marie Roth	32	33	121
Len Rotondaro	47	83	120
Frank J. Rubesky		31	55
Laurie Rudman		86	102
Donna S. Rutsky			101
Dawn E. Rutter			67
Pat St. Pierre		24	104
Virgie McCoy Sammons			43
Mary Lou Sanelli			111
Christopher P. Sanger			80
Jean Sangster			68
Mary Saracino		34	109
Joan C. Sauer		79	123
John T. Savino			118
Robert J. Savino		45	86
John A. Scarffe		39	95
Gary A. Scheinoha		91	102
Terry Scheinoha			88
Margaret L. Schell		55	118
Maryann M. Schingo			66
Barry P. Schmidt			92
Susan Schmidt			65
David C. Schrader			73
Alan Schueler			70
Ruth Wildes Schuler		56	69
Linda Jean Schutz			44
Nancy K. Schwager		53	94
Don Sears		42	124
Rick Sears			115
Janice Seaver		87	120
Greg Senn			113
Dennis Share			44
Louise Sharrock		37	91
Harry B. Sheftel		96	121
Candace Gonzalez Shelton		81	123
Maurice Shumpert			58
Rosemary Siders		111	113

* New Worlds 1981 Poetry Contest winning poem.

*Images
of the
Mystic Truth*

NEW WORLDS 1981 POETRY CONTEST

Contest #1:   FUNNY POEM

First Place: Hannah Fox

MEANWHILE, BACK ON EARTH

Astronomers and physicists
And surgeons, I exalt
Your genius, your discoveries,
Your logic free of fault.

I read with avid interest of
Your naked singularities,
Your black holes, neutron stars and all
Those other cosmic rarities.

Before my wondering eyes you make
The universe unfold -
But right now I'd be more impressed
If you could cure my cold!

SQUELCHED

Was he joking, that man of mine,
Or was he drinking too much wine?
"I want my body burned," he said.
"Please grant my wish when I am dead.
My ashes shall be scattered near
Upon these hills I hold so dear."

He pressed me for a solemn vow.
I shut him up and this is how:
"I'll do your bidding if I must
And think of you each time I dust."

Second Place:
Erna G. Brown
(left)

Honorable Mention:
Elizabeth Whitbeck
(right)

LAISSEZ FAIRE

The laws have relaxed,
taboos have shrunk,
more pleasures are taxed,
more people are drunk.
What was forbidden before
is now acceptable;
what we used to deplore
is no longer disreputable.
The world is a playground
and we are all free
in an atmosphere of pollution
and mounting debris,
knowing full well
each life-enhancer
will kill our brain cells
or give us cancer.

First Place: Dorothy Corbett Gentleman

ELEGY

Music dribbled out of his pockets,
dissolving like smoke onto leaves
already chlorophylled for the new
symphonies of bird song.

Together our tongues
would have memorized each other
for the long silence,
but his single voice
dimmed like an ending parade.

I remember lip-reading his small sounds
while the rhythm of his fingers
made a constant hum over white skin,
his feet pushing open the night.

Alone I fill the cracks in my heart
with left-over wind and sun.
I listen to rattling twigs,
the chanting of boughs,
the rustle of my skirt
murmuring half a duet
with the droppings from my punctured eyes.

PROM NIGHT

Amid a flurry of laces and frills
sisters attire her for Prom night
as brother secretly shovels pine-
needle earth, a forest grave, last
cradle for her cat, only companion.
Pretty pleas elicit mascara from Mom;
he finally closes mystical green eyes
that held the universal secrets.
Warm joy over layers of pink tulle
erase distress over a missing ribbon,
stolen by a brother, bow for his burden.
Cinderella receives a wrist corsage,
roses and ribboned hearts and pearls;
he lays Persephone flowers, purloined
spring violets across a forest bed
nestling the box that once held pink
satin slippers for a daydream sister
too fragile for midnight revelations
that 'Stairway to Heaven' is cardboard
and crepe paper, a lesson as lonely
as unborn kittens and their mother
in the moss of forever sleep.

NOTES FROM WITHIN

I am lying in my bed waiting
for the sleeping poppies to do their magic.
No thoughts are whirling like dust in my brain.
The seasons, the years evaporate.

This room used to hold four corners.
It is a place where hours are measured
by pills in a bottle, where bombs
are disguised as finger-fuses, and
retroactive scars sear like footfalls.
Tears burn the wallpaper.
In my mind, I carve the room to fit,
parting the doors like the lips of a wound.

Meanwhile, I am drifting down the Nile,
into a quiet sleep of no real distance.
This is the best way to travel.
I am no longer haunted by walls,
windows, and family bibles.

I have always been greedy about sleep.
Each night, I place these stones
on heart and throat,
in order to drown with my hands sewn
into the lining of my own coat.

First Place: Alice Mackenzie Swaim

VICTORIAN LANDSCAPE

Where are the ladies on the summer lawns,
languid in garden chairs, with lemonade,
arranged like flowers in a patch of shade
and waiting for men's coming, when there dawns
a re-awakening innocence that spawns
desire in every cool, sequestered glade?
Where is the silent, white-capped serving maid,
the children, fate's small hostages and pawns?
We have no time now for such leisured ease;
trim gardens wear a hurried carefulness,
no flagstoned pathways under ancient trees,
nor gravelled walkways for parentheses.
How did it happen? By what slow degrees
did we exchange acceptance for duress?

ON HIS TWENTY-FIRST BIRTHDAY

Now days can pass without a thought of you.
How else can one regard an adult son?
You have your goals and dreams you must pursue
And my imperfect nurturing is done.
So I have built a fortress to inure
Myself from wanting you at home where I
Might keep you, lessen you, and so insure
A wheezing pekingese or a bonsai.
But under seige of memort my fort
Collapses, just a battlement of sand
Attacked by waves, a hillock left as ort,
And all my good intentions cannot stand.
     So I return with bucket and tin spade
     To build your monument, my barricade.

Second Place:

Betty Downing

(left)

CHIMERA

Always one and one it seems
Broken lives and broken dreams
Eyes that cry a bloodless tear
Mouths that echo whispered fear

What's my answer -- puzzles blend
Lost beginning's tempting end
Promised peace or voided bleak
hollow spaces dark and deep

Drift away in smoky mists
above the darting fateful twists
Wondrous hues ethereal glow
lilting songs that few can know

Chimera, muse, in shattered thought
Travelers lost before we sought
the lapse of times' pursuing probe
searching out the soul of Job

Honorable Mention:

Judith E. Hannan

(right)

First Place: Rebecca S. Rossignol

PINE

Overhanging pine...
Your needles meet the water
Rafts for daring ants

Second Place: Clo Weirich

UNTITLED

Transformation
Snow glyphics
etch
Sturdy cyclone fence
changing it
to a neo - Picasso

Honorable Mention: Cheryl L. Henderson

FOG

This is like driving through sleep
with its secrets.

The earth is breathing
giving back to the sky
its gift of water,
giving us this mystery.

IN THE NAME OF LOVE

First Place: Mark McNease

HIATUS AT MAIN AND EUCLID

Fingers don't reach the crossing,
No wrungs real or imagined,
And without fingers there is no touch.

You've withdrawn through the keyhole
Your door exposes, creating a hiatus
At Main and Euclid, our small chasm.

Only the names have been changed
To protect the geometric neighborhood, all nice houses.
We glare here. We ruffle feathers and bedposts.

I glue pieces of the dismantle while you
Doze or fix on tubular images.
The idiot box. Is that where we live?

That hiatus from fact to magic,
The warmth of fire and its inaccessible draw?
Burning takes precedence with such heat.

Fingers don't cross the reaching,
No hand holds true or concocted,
And without fingers there is no touch.

We sling honed words like glass shards
In the name of love, calling it honesty,
Calling it the inevitable expanse of growth

Like blood around an opening.
One of us will sleep unfit and the other
Crawl down this hiatus to its incurable bottom.

LIFE LINES

they read tea leaves
in the bottom of tea cups
I too look for patterns of promise
life's cup drunk to the dregs
in cryptic configuration
your face my fortune

Third Place: Laurette Houle Gutierrez

LAST LOVE

There were no stars the night you were born.
The sky is empty again tonight. Blank. Undemanding.
You say I am not the right one.
But the resemblance is close, so you surrender.
Parts of longings, glances, habits you can't lose,
lay on your grate: backed up.
I am there, too-- endlessly resurrected--
the childhood religion you can't shake.
You see now, that the best years of your life
are not still to come. Wind into your fabric
like a beekeeper. Curl against me again, a pilot
caught in a drift. This is what we wait for:
Something to say.

WINTER HEARTS

I cannot love this much winter
we are cold
two hearts of snow.

If I could touch you
would the winter turn to spring?

I know:
I was the one who longed for autumn
(summer fire was too intense, near the end).

It seemed safe to fall to you,
the reddest apple,
but when I bit
you only teased
& turned to snow.

No
I cannot love this much winter
I sigh for spring,
say it will come.

AN ENCINITAS MORNING

Brooding its life in the sleep of Spanish tile & heavy trees,
The faint gray walls of silent houses lighten in the early morning sky.
Ripe, purple avocados plop to the ground.
As my shadow hurries down the street,
I walk fast, trying to catch up to the breaking day.
Birds chirp a chorus of clear sounds-
Hidden from sight, a rooster crows.
I might mistake the sights & sounds for a Mediterranean paradise,
But, no-
It's the breath of beauty in Encinitas.

Cynthia Wolfer

LAKE VERMILLION SUNSET

The sun is a light going out
on the other side of Lake Vermillion.
The boats are silhouettes,
the people in them shadows.
Their voices are sharper than their vague outlines
But still only echoes.....
in the center of the lake they watch the sunset.
The lake calms with the darkness.....
Like a child going to sleep.

Valerie J. Olson

BEHIND THE BROWNSTONES ON GROVE STREET

There are patches of grass where
Cities of blueberries grow wild against the bricks.
Each small fruit fights for the sunlight;
-Most survive!! It's the law of this land,
The beauty of the village!

Cyndi Ellen Baer

UNTITLED

A picture may be worth
a thousand
words,
but a touch goes
far beyond.
The simplest form
of communication,
expression.
The purest poetry.
A gentle whisper
that knows no other
language.

Barbara Klapperich

YANG

the first bird's song
cracks the dark egg
and reveals the dawn

Charles Lance Fox

13

EXPLORE

We seem to share a mutual respect
for the open space of nature.
I wish to give to you a gift,
an extension of my being
of size enough to arena your needs.

Between you and me
there exists a free and open wilderness
encompassing a vast amount of passion,
infinite desires,
endless dreams.

Somewhere out in this vast and boundless
sphere,
We will openly, freely express ourselves
to one another.

Explore with me.

Shirley Ann Hipp

HANZEL

Dawn Hanzel, but always
the tiny throb
of swallow flight

that crayon scrawl
of air and wing
flapping the dust magically

erasing each of your steps
even before you have taken them.

Robert J. Oberg

A LIBATION TO THE GOD OF PEACE
(To Roy Cadwell, Founder,
Lester B. Pearson Peace Park)

Lord, that I could capture
The flutter of every wing
Seizing all the rapture
Of each transparent thing,

Gathering to my breast
Without wherefore or why
The hearts of all the best
To raise up to the sky

an infinite offering,

Then would I ever cease
To sleep with open eye
Having given tears of peace
To flood the earth on high?

Janet Pembor

FRAGILE MOMENTS

I wrote to you in happier times.
Into each letter, a little part of my heart
Was chiseled away as I wrote words of love.
My soul was laid bare to you.
Now my letters are fragments
Of my sorrowing heart and hopeless tears.
I ask nothing in return...
And in these last sad years
I speak softly of my love...
Yet no one hears.

Mary Stickley Feagans

14

SOUVENIRS

When they cut the trees
in Tennessee they
used to find sparks
hidden in the tight wood.

Bullets son my father
said from the war.
A layer of lead lay
in the wood, held in time,
growing with the tree
until a sharper saw was born.

I would lie in bed
and wonder if
those men knew
what their bullets did, the ones that missed.

Fred. W. Wright Jr.

MY MORNING CHILD

The morning of your lifetime
brought a shadow to my stance.
Your shady patch would follow
in our fully measured dance.
Companion of the daybreak
will diminish when the sun
crosses the meridian
and I will stand as one.
I see the dawn extending,
growing into afternoon.
My shade appearing smaller;
midday has come too soon.

Caroly Poe

A STRAIGHT PATH

I closed my eyes
And I saw everything
More clearly than if they were open
My body groped in the darkness
But my mind knew the way
And It followed a straight path
To enlightenment

Gregory Liffick

UNSUNG

You run through me
like a wistful song,
whose melody cries
within the matter of my mind
and whose lyrics taste
the edge of my lips
with words too sad to sing.

Caroly Poe

A SPIDER'S LABOR

The poor spider
Spins her beautiful work of art
In a futile attempt to please the Dawn.
But, alas, Dawn awakens
And sprinkles the spider's work of art
With her tears of joy.
The spider rests peacefully
She knows that when Dawn is at her peak
And sun peers over the blanket of night
Her work of art will be finished
With the soft glaze of Sun's radiant smile

Dawn Myers

UNTITLED

Certain things can bring to mind
 memories of a forgotten time.
Tarnished scenes of days gone by.
 The two of us. Just you and I.

Little things that meant so much.
 Faded photos. A film of dust
now covers treasures we once held dear.
 Their value lessens with passing years.

But now and then I sort them out
 remembering things we talked about.
It's harder as the years go by.
 We once were close. Just you and I.

Alana Lally

THURSDAY

Winter coerces autumn's
Sweet departure
In a snowy horse-driven carriage;
And there is a certain weeping
Heard above the howling wind.
The lost grey thrush
Condemns the wicked ice which
Hangs like a presage
From the very edges of an
Even darker morning.
Volte-face!
At last, the barren magnolia
Comforts a vagabond
Other than me.

Diana Kwiatkowski

A FAITHFUL COMPANION

So many years we've been together,
in cloudy, sunny, and stormy weather.
You've stood by my side early and late;
while I smiled or cried or pondered my fate.
A silent companion indeed you've been;

you keep my secrets better than a closest friend.
When I've stood by you tired and sad, you were always the same,
never sad or mad.
When I leaned on you for rest and strength,
you bore me up with never a complaint.
As the years wore on you weakened in frame;
but your companionship was always the same.
But, now, my dear friend, in spite of all we've been through;
I simply must buy another IRONING BOARD that's new!

Bertha Mayes

TRIBUTE TO JOHNNY BOY

How sad is truth that at fifteen and just happening
Along its shores, the Hudson River lured you
Into its depths, its quiet beauty of frozen snow
Hypnotically beckoning seemed a challenge for diving in.
But broken talons of ice carried you down down
Freezing you in your valiant struggle for survival,
And silently you went into its rapid currents,
Into its gushing oblivion.
In its broken mirrors there were no messages.

And now as we stand over your grave,
Father, Mother, all those who loved you,
We pray that one day it will be you beckoning to each of us.
And in that calmest sea of Heaven,
Once again we shall all be together!

                    Franco Buono

THE MEASURE

The poets see beyond the veil
That covers all reality.
They put in words the songs of heart,
And picture life for all to see.

The poets flourish with the arts
When freedom cuts the chains of thought
And lets the mind roam through the skies
And ponder ideas that it sought.

It must be true that any age,
When measured by its poets' voice,
Will show the depth of freedom's roots
And prove if mind has any choice.

        Jo Starrett Lindsey

TO HART CRANE
(After reading about his death)

Take the gift so soon
Which others sought
Into the watery death
Of moon-deep sleep.

It may diffuse a power
Too painful to keep,
The dream never fulfilled,
The soul lost to men.

Keep the gift within,
Not to spill too many drops
Onto paper to remember
Not to breathe too deep.

            Nancy Barrett

AFTER DON JUAN

Crossing godless streets, traversed but not inhabited
We frequent cafes, coffee shops, to drink without tasting
Eat without partaking, make love without loving; having
Stroked godless hearts, palm against polyester
Lips against loneliness; against heartless gods
Our emptiness rails.

We clean soiled hands in Market Street johns
Baptize yellowed teeth with Sambos caffeine
While the tattered-suited man scores the sidewalk
  behind Denny plastic flowers
He too, an aloneness-fighter, glows with his lighter, his
Scavenged butts burn briefly and die a second death;
We too (but inside) court death with our women --
First death in the conquest, the second at sunrise.

Philip Clayton

PROMETHEUS

Someone will come someday
and leash my freedom to his fame.
Some lucky man, scarcely human,
clear-eyed with an unworried body,
will make me his opportunity.
He will never have seen failure;
my chains and birds of prey are
doves and strings for his toys.
And so, grown used to renown
as the consequence of his acts,
unthinkingly, he will free me.

Dear child, grow up soon;
your guilty father waits for you.

James Cesarano

ONE TO KNOW

It
is
remarkable
to
be
well
known.
It
is
more
worthy
to
know
yourself.

James Terry Foster

MY MASK

Leave it by the bed.
I wear it everywhere.
It's just that your fingers
stroked me so slowly, so warmly,
that I didn't notice when
you eased it off. My face
must be pale and frightened.
Yours is.

I fling the mirror you hand me
against a wall. Briefly silver
rains on your carpet. I won't look
at a woman who hides nothing.

Pat Mora

18

WHEN I'M A COURT REPORTER

When I'm a court reporter, I'll dine
        in expensive vegetarian restaurants
Now I stir-fry bok-choy to satisfy my wants.
I'll buy New Balance running shoes, when now my Nike's suffice
        I'll own that Orvis rod I love and camp out on the ice.
There'd be no greater pleasure than fishing all day long
        to hurl in gorgeous rainbow trout
                while breaking into song.
When I'm a court reporter, I'll be making loads of money
        to enjoy the finer things in life
                like the Appalachians so sunny.
The day is coming soon, I know, I'll pass that CSR --
Too bad there aren't courtrooms
        in the forests wide and far.

                                Kathy Morrone

SPIDER WEB

Sometimes we couldn't laugh,
A spider spins his web in earnest,
and a moth flies with dizzying determination.

Love was a word used sparingly.
The web was slow in construction,
and quick to break.

I fluttered into your clever netting
as any moonstruck moth would do.
You delicately untangled and had me

in your soft silk, then let me go.
I am caught now in the pristine freedom of air
that brings your vibrations even now, alluring me.

                Ruth Laine

PASSIVE

My pen rests idle
beside the paper-pad
awaiting thoughts to write.

My brain rests idle
on my pillow-pad
awaiting thoughts to write.

        My hands rest idle
        on the pen...
        paper-pad remains
                lily-white.

                Goldia Y. Ball

19

WITHIN AND WITHOUT

Radio blaring, Gong Show on the TV
Family, friends, the turmoil of company

Speaking, smiling, lying, misplaced sincerity
Hiding, dodging, masking, unseen is the real me

Ugly shell, sand stained, cracked, ocean worn
Unattached, vulnerable, in two pieces I'm torn

Shut the door, dim the light, tighten shutters
Find a chair, still the mind, Forget all others

Music, sweet symphony, images on a screen
Perception, reflections, the richness of that unseen

Quieting, listening, silencing, discovered serenity
Awaken, return, function, use nurtured abilities

Painted shell, mortared crack, sand swept free
Within and without now sing in harmony

Larry Giarrizzo

STORM

City windows are closed
Tight as canning jars
Kitchen lights flash on and off.
Grey rolling clouds threaten to dance
Into a whirlwind tornado.
Spaces between cloud masses
Show bruised colors...
purple, grey and mud-yellow...
Like a black eye from a bar-room brawl.

Valerie J. Olson

RAINFALL

Like a continuous
Falling teardrop
The rain crashes to earth
Unhampered
Unhurried, unreluctant
I lie under shelter
Of a warm roof
And I glory in its rhythm

Gregory Liffick

UNTITLED

Old people
are like bottles
of ketchup.

You have to
shake them up and then
have lots of
patience.

Phyllis Yang

NIGHT LIFE

I behold
the insomnia of trains
whistling through the valley
during the darkest hours
and catfights in alleyways
long after bars have closed,
and the place
where elves and fairies dance
beneath the ring around the moon.

Barbara Pearson

20

SONNET TO A KITTEN

Soft trembling and shy, it came to me
Wide eyes staring at the world, and I
Knew that the new-born blue-stare could not see. . .
My heart reached out to hear the plaintive cry
Of hunger. Then soft nuzzling in my hand
It cuddled, quickly nursing all the milk
That drop by drop increased its tiny span;
The fur so warm, soft like a layered silk.
This tiny spark of life I gently held;
It purred and breathed, close-pressed against my face --
My heart was moved, was tender-touched -- and dwelled
A part of me. Then in my days a space
   Was sweetly filled and strangely warmed by this
   Small mite of life, God's unexpected bliss.

              Paul K. McAfee

TENDER

eyes
quiet
gentling
to
rush...
skin
in
glow
to
flames
of
hush...

Love
blush...

      Michael L. Adams

PORTRAIT

The careless
curtain of hair,
faint sensual
smile,
untroubled eyes
with a deeper
hint of
madness.

This pose is
well rehearsed;
your name is
Sylvia too.

  Gloria H. Procsal

MONDAY--3A.M.

In a kiss of absolution we moved
with erotic apologies into each other's arms,
the tender war of flesh taking precedence
above the well-honed daggers of our words.

The delicate tongue-lashing I received
was nothing like the vicious verbal one preceding,
seeming instead to lap at the open wounds
that had been so callously inflicted.

As your hand traced my breast, its honeyed salve
spread slowly in the bleeding gashes so finely drawn--
they will be sealed in ephemeral lines
and glisten in the light like spider webs.

              Kit Carlson

21

TIMELESS GRACE

Fleeting gusts of wind
span across the eternal source
from whence they come and go.
Leaves in the trees shiver from the breeze
of a warm summer's day - as they look down
upon the flowers of the meadow
swaying to the music
of a silent wind instrument.

Swept up in its current
the dust is scattered for miles
across the burning sands of the deserts;
while high in the mountains
an Eagle rides the waves
of timeless grace.

Philip J. Kokinis

FOR MY BELOVED

I touch your ring of gold
then remember the man I wed
in spite of
bayonets
firebombs
and hate

Today I weep
with our child
for your poor shattered
mind
and the cruel world of
shadows
in which you are doomed
to live.

Dawn Langley Simmons

FIERCE

Oh young one,
This flesh of us
Is an animal thing,
One bite
    And the pull
Encompassing.
We
  Are Pegasi in flight,
Satin black
        And linen white,
Winging through this murkiness of cloud
As so many stilettos
Piercing
    An Aegean fog.

John Mueller

STILTED ILLUSIONS

Ironing boards give wrinkled hallucinations.
They shadow our visions and consequence.
Heated thought waves bend an ear to our minds
as we constantly press our existence.

Thomas J. Anderson III

UNTITLED

Eternal poundings of surf
Carrying the sun upon its back
To shore
Drenching the coast
With promises from the sea.

Lori Lewis

GATHERERS

The world is thick and horrendous
With smooth-talking smilers
Looking for your loyalty.
They will strip you
To the bone
And leave you shining and friendless.
Beware, beware
Their sleek, pretty faces will greet you
With love on their lips.
They worship the great god I.
There is a strict accounting
Of all that is received.
You will be called upon
To pay.

                    Isabel Marshall

WAITING, WATCHING

I have waited all these many years
Watching, watching from beneath my brows
So many figures, so many faces
Ah, so many beautiful faces...

But a man grows cold from waiting
And his eyes so dark by watching

I would forget all those many years
And watch just you with open eyes
If you would slip your arms about me
And with your fragile hands caress me...

I would give you all I have
And forget what other faces gave.

                    Erich Krueger

CAT UP A TREE

"Come down," I say.
        "I can't," says she.
"Why not?" ask I.
        Her reply?
        "I'm up a tree."

"I know!" I shout.
        "Then help," cries she.
"How?" ask I.
        Her reply?
        "Come rescue me."

"Come, get me down," she carries on.
        "Are you nuts?!" to her from me.
"Get a ladder and get me down!"
        My reply?
        "Go climb a tree."

                    Beth Franz

WILD LEAVES

Are there not wild leaves
with passions blown
darkly wet against the earth
that grieve of trees
they've known and loved at birth
that in some small green way
one may not surmise
(yet gracious God may hear)
die petalling the day
with their unspoken cries?

                    Gail Razinsky

MARRIED

You have tied the knot,
And I remain bound in Freedom.

Do you pity the old maid?
I am no old maid.
Love- much have I had and lost,
given and retained.
I am no old maid.

Have you forgotten the day the rain
Trapped Us in the country
And baptized Us at once
Together?
Fluidity in union,
Divorced from entanglement...

Have you become twisted in your knot?

                    Barbara Burgower

FROM COCOON TO BUTTERFLY

Slamming the door you abruptly leave,
A part of you remains:
memories.

There is no emotional feeling.
A butterfly spreads its wings as the
whistling wind brings coldness.
Spring flowers and innocence
are not to blame.

Curled in the middle of the bed
your small son sleeps.

                    Pat St. Pierre

TOUCHING THE CLOUDS

In my dreams again,
I tread the soaring kame,
And slide down strawberry banks,
To Mallory's verdant velvet edge.

I fish the silver waters;
Then tiptoeing softly
Seek the hiding druids,
In Milton's mossy woods.

When twilight approaches,
I tap at Mother's door,
In togetherness we review
My wondrous visitations.

                    Ida M. Lister McLaughlin

THE DICE WERE ONE

It was a complete
                and final triumph,
But there was no concern,
No healthy pleasure.

You can try and contest it,
But the string of music would
Perhaps make you intensely happy,
                For no reason at all.

You were innocent and incorrigible,
                But lasted for how long,
And who remained the winner,
                When the dice were one?

                    Frank Atanacio

24

AUGUST, A BEE, YOU, AND ME

As Summer shortens in twilight,
Lounging in anticipation
                    of crisp
Autumn,
          Stickpin bumbling-bees
Reminisce on the face
Of upturned sunflowers, sun-burnt
Brown surrounded by brittle
Reproof.
Under incandescence, in
Diffusing light spread over
                    A Lone Table
On spare brown carpet,
Thoughts of you on white sheets strewn
In a circle.

                    Kent Glenzer

TRITE TALK

My mother told me
it was inappropriate to
talk peace at the dinner table.
She said it was also unsuitable
to speak peace at social
gatherings like cocktail parties
or church and school assemblies.
My mother told me it was rude
to read poetry to my sister
when the television was on.
She told me to destroy my poetry, for
no one wanted to hear about the bomb.
And when I told her it was love,
she ignored me and blabbed on.

                    Libby Hubbard

STRAW BOATS

Keep grabbin' them floating straws
Pretty soon you'll have enough
to weave yourself a boat,
but just make damn sure
you know how much weight
it'll carry before you go in
push it into Neptune's Pond.

Sometimes you confuse myths
with real things, so listen!
Straw boats are risky, even
if the grass is tight.
But loose braids without
pitch ain't no proper boat
it's just a good way t'drown.

                    W.O. Wacaster

THE WIND AT PLAY

Skimming in endless rolls
Lofting to heights, tumbleweeds,
Like balls bounced by arms
Of the wind...
Begins an endless journey.

The playful wind sleeps
The air grows silent.
Leaving rootless companions
Clutching, restlessly rolling
Waiting, waiting for the awakening
Of the playful wind.
When they will be lifted
Toward the sky again.

                    Dorothy E. Colvert

dear one

standing there in front of my building
holding on
to each other

your eyes asking me if I'll be o.k.
and something so gentle about you that I want to keep forever

our hands parting for the last time
because of worlds and words we have talked over

and now, I wonder
like the first lines of a letter
how you've been

the content is scattered
it could be anyone

the end says I miss you

Mozelle Dayan

DEATH

Always airports
always goodbyes
always striving
always reaching
for and beyond
the sky.
And now it is yours.
goodbye

Joyce Randolph

UNTOUCHED

I have never picked a flower in bud,
 nor plucked a fruit before its time.
It always seems to taste the best
 as it's about to drop from the vine.
The primitive attraction
 of clear, cold mountain streams
 or the virgin snows
             from which they feed.
Isolated,
     hidden from man's mad rush,
     the most beautiful things in life
     are those untouched.

David Benson

THE DANCE

I have dreamed
I have risked it all
danced with failure
but still kept right on dancing
a step or two lost
but quickly recovered
we all miss a beat sometime
we all lose our balance somewhere
but the music plays on
and so long as I hear the music
I must dance

Kathy Keogh

26

THE POET KNOWS

With agonizing drops of time,
A meaningless pebble the poet sees,
Growing with eternity's trying patience,
An aging rock, full fledged to trip over.
Don't fall, step gently over it.
A little more, the pebble's a boulder,
Now seen, down a path still rolling.
Can't miss, don't get caught up,
Let go to make it better.
It's finished, don't make it tower,
The pebble, a mile high mountain,
Just look, don't touch again.
It's perfect, and the poet knows.

                    Brenda Ledbetter

WORDS

An unkind word spoken
Went speeding on its way,
Lodged in a tender heart
Left scars destined to stay.

A Kind word spoken
Sped upon its way,
Lodged in a broken heart
Mended it that very day.

Lord, give me kindly words
To reach an aching heart,
And never unkind words
That pierce like a poison dart.

                    Hazel L. Davis

THE MOURNER

They are not shadows;
They are bruises that lift the shallow light
From her face, as she backs slowly away from the body
Pale and still on the bed.
The faded sheet she had wound herself in
To hide her nakedness,
Falls to the floor, useless.

In the warm, bloodlight of dawn
Her body begins to shiver slightly,
And she laughs; at first gently, queerly,
Then in spasms and ejaculations, choking and gasping,
Until her body aches and shudders and the tears come.
He had taught her to laugh when in pain:
Now, as she stares at the body, she cannot stop. She cannot.

                    John Terlesky

IF

If I were God
I would not trod
On unsure sod.

     Floyd M. Regan, Jr.

27

SURVIVORS IN THE BACK FIELD

Summer's end, and time to slay these shoots,
Upstarts in my pastures, nuisance things,
Persimmon, sumac, hickory. Each one clings
To earth in stubborn hold. It seems their roots
Get stronger, tougher every year, and all's
To do is fight back, stubborn, too. I'll lay
You low, bale wreckers, thieves of my good hay!
The time is right when every growing thing falls
Half-asleep. Seems I get cut down too when
Least alert. And yet a pruning just then
Forces hardier growth, makes for a spreading
Out, and at the core, a toughening.
Brother Weed, root of my root, face to
My blade. Worthy enemy, I salute you!

                    Barbara Hurd

ROSEBUD

The ghost of age sits on my father's brow;
these years my mother only dreams of sin.
We pal about the old and weathered plow,
no worries, for I am nine and you but ten.
Quick in our world of jeans and party dresses;
now is the day we race the sun over hills,
my hand in yours, I chase your long limp tresses.
We push old age aside: we have no ills.
Someday your shape will beguile men's lust eyes;
but then, my girl, your face will wither dry.
Though I, a fool, will fool women with lies,
somehour I will lose my boyish charm and die.
And we will turn to clay so soiled in earth,
rosebud, we were born racing from our birth.

                    Rusty Standridge

TO WITNESS WITHIN

A thought in the morning
Over a cheery tune
Came again at dark
To witness within--
There is little
Love doesn't know.

          Sheryl Williams

A POEM

  is a poem-
  is a poem
until one reads it
        and finds within
  a dream-
    a vision-
    a memory
lost in the
      tumble of mind
    waiting patiently
      to be found
                and remembered.

              Karen DeGroot

SO SOON

Light comes to us
Within a second -
Yet Death,
Surely the fastest thing,
Takes a lifetime
Till it beckons.

  B. Wayne Zajac

28

ELLIS ISLAND

Ellis Island, in New York, the port
Of freedom for all those who sought entry
Into a better world. Of every sort
Of men they came. The rich, landed gentry.
The poor, dispossessed, to them the sentry
Of liberty called with beckoning glow.
New life, high hope wherever they might go.
And some took trains to Western States afar,
Their children and all earthly goods aboard,
To find lush land and grassy plains. Their star
Led them to quiet homes. Gentle reward
For lives of previous toil. Others restored
Their past remaining in the busy town
Where they found peace, and many gained renown.

                    Mary Frances Langford

WOULD YOU HAVE LAUGHED?

Where are you now that time has had its way?
Does happiness or sorrow rule your day?
Have you too felt the loneliness and tears
That cling to me unceasing all the years?
That summer moment when we chanced to meet,
Endures within my spirit sad and sweet.
I touched your hand! My soul is trembling still.
One touch was all, a whole life to fulfill.
The moment quivered, faltered, and was gone,
The memory sweet and sensuous as the dawn.
My lips were silent, though my thoughts were bold.
I stood entranced--my terror was controlled.
If I had voiced my silent plea that day,
Would you have laughed and gone about your way?

                    Wayne Nelson

AT THE DIAMOND MINES

We turn our gaudy find,
hold it to the light,
dull it with eager sweat.

Each alluvial facet
scorches like prisoned fire,
inflames our eyes

until some computed mind,
robot-like,
condemns it as common stone.

More blind than before,
we bend again to clay feet,
frantic, searching for gems.

                    Evelyn Corry Appelbee

VESSEL OF LOVE

Take my body
into your hands.
Then,
ever so gently,
mold it into a chalice.
Pour into it,
the wisdom of your youth,
the honey of my ages.
Then,
sip from it slowly
and leave but a taste,
of the love of all ages.

                    Vicki Augustine

DECEMBER MIRAGE

I love the Christmas season
When folks forget a while
The troubles that beset them,
And take the time to smile.

I love the Christmas season
When people become friends;
When they feel a kinship;
Take time to make amends.

I love the Christmas season
When an ordinary street
Turns into magic fairyland,
While into childhood we retreat.

Oh, I love the Christmas season
And the gladness it imparts,
But isn't it a pity,
After New Years it departs?

                Wanda B. Blaisdell

OVER

His skin felt hot on the lips caressing it,
And she began to feel the familiar wave of excitement,
But, he was not responding.
His expression:
Certain, yet lackluster eyes and lips in a casual clench
:showed utter indifference.
The words came slowly and deliberately,
As if he were giving an oration to the Roman masses.
And he told her, in a manner as cool as the blade that killed Caesar,
He didn't love her.

                Lynn Moore

RAIN

Springtime rain has magical powers
That bring new life to dormant flowers
As gentle raindrops softly fall
A rose bush forms a scarlet wall.

                Joseph M. Pallozzi

PHANTASY

Sickness pervades the cloistered sphere
this world he calls his own.
Mutterings leap with meanings unclear
crying a message unknown.

Shadowy thoughts revoke the day
God gave His hand, then turned away.

Come see the shell that isn't a man,
muse at this poor wretched fool.
Look to his eyes a moment and then
depart his mad vestibule.

                Walter Trizna

FRIENDSHIP IN PROSE

There is a price tag on almost everything in this world,
With exception .... One cannot buy a true friend!
One can rent an acquaintance .. or get an enemy free.
A true friend may be had through reciprocal feeling, or luck.
Acquaintances can be counted by the dozens; whereas,
Friends are counted on the fingers of one hand -- or less.
But be careful -- A Friendship has great fragility:
If it is dropped, it may break;
Or if abandoned, it will wither away!
Guard it constantly with extreme care --
The reward will last a lifetime.

Frank J. Rubesky

SNOOKY-SEA AND DING-A-LING

Snooky-Sea met Ding-A-Ling
    A crazy mixed-up little thing.
So off they went to see the fair ..
    The carousel and scenic there.

Snooky-Sea set out to show
    That he knew how the roosters crowed:
Since it was night then lift the light
    And torch our way across this sight.

Ding-A-Ling shot balloons bright
    And won a doggie that didn't bite.
Now she has a little pet
    To help her with her table set.

With dimples round and a tiny crown
Ding seemed to move the world around.

Joe Gleason Jr.

UNTITLED

So you're here again
With your monthly phone calls
And the diag gossip
And the grapevine messages
And my dreams
    ...of love
    ...of spite
    ...of future
    and past.
I think so hard about forgetting
That I can't stop
Remembering!
What a beautiful day
When you finally leave
My mind
And I'm free to love again
And be your friend.

Wendy Bittker

WILD INDIAN NAMES

I love to hear wild Indians' names:
Touch the Clouds, Man Afraid,
Hole in the Day.
I am but a soliloquist!

Iron Thunder, Conquering Bear,
He Who Has Been Everywhere.
Where have they all gone?

The Shooting Star once blazed a path,
Then faded in the night.

Came Crazy Horse of Custer fame:
"Remember the children," he said,
And soon he was dead.

Their voices now are stilled,
No promises fulfilled.

I love to hear wild Indians....

James Dowd

DEATH OF VIOLETS

Here lie violets, on the mound,
sore where the roots would be.
Someone stole them from the stem
and deserted them on the mound.
They cry and ache for attention.

Here, lies Violet, under the mound, sore.
She stole herself from life.
She cried and ached for attention.
She hated violets.

Lee Smith

BLACK IS MY WORLD TODAY

Black is my world today
Flat empty skies,
Dropping hot burning angel tears
Worms wiggle in black stinking mud
Wallowing in orgasmic ecstasy.

Black are my thoughts today
Strangled emotion
Whirling in howling nothingness
Fall into a poet's pit
Eternal night of my own making.

Katherine Lithgow

DIRECTIONS; WATER WITH LOVE

A flower without water
Dies a horrible death.

You cannot hear it screaming
It hasn't any breath.

Don't neglect this flower
I'm holding out to you.

People's deepest regrets
Are for things they never knew.

Don L. White

UNTITLED

Between life and death
There is but a single breath
Choose to love me now.

Rose Marie Roth

TIME, AND TIME AGAIN

Silly words - sure
but they were special, too.
Certainly no other person
in the whole universe
had such luck
as I, to hear him whisper,
"Sweetest girl, you're my baby duck."

Selves abandon times
of youth and tender fires.
Reality pleats the face
and words no longer private
stuff my ear.
His message now loudly spoken,
"Hey, Waddles, how about a beer?"

June Lee Humphrey

THE STORM

My whole being vibrates
    to the symphonic notes of a melody,
A rubato song played by
    tossing tree branches...
Wind-blown agitated clouds
    staccato chords of thunder
        syncopated glissando of lightning.
Exhilarating concerto of nature
    played fortissimo in a major key.
Within the discordant tune my soul finds
    a reassuring andante melody.
My heart hears the contrapuntal song
    your heart has written to me.
Hears gratefully and is at peace!

Alexandra J. Prober

GREEN ROOFTOP

Green rooftop
Newly painted for the winter ahead
A coat for protection
You're damp
Dew from the trees
An autumn perspiration
Wind freezes your moisture
Making a shiny, slick, shattering,
Cold experience
For the leaves huddling
On you

Gary Jedinak

8/4/80

Do broken hearts ever mend?
Can they be repaired or replaced?
Or are they just discarded,
Leaving an empty space?

That's what it feels like.
There's no beating, no thumping,
Just an empty hole.
Not even a dull ache
It matches my empty soul.

Glenda Anderson-Parker

UNTITLED

Do you see my trees?
The silver moon slips through them.
I cannot follow.

Rose Marie Roth

33

NEW YEAR'S DAY

Awake! A beam electrifies and lifts
The soul above the clouds to mountain heights.
Across the skies are blazing New Year gifts,
Exploding arcs of brightly colored lights.

This instant cuts the binding bonds of old,
And creates dawn for hopeful souls who know
Ahead are fruitful fields of green and gold,
And campfires warm with everlasting glow.

Midst mellowed grain, atop this sunward crest,
I'd wish to live, with every dream fulfilled.
Aside from harvests' yield and hilltop zest,
I shall seek God, to do what He has willed.

When bounty, sun, and summit disappear,
The lasting beacon, God, will still be near.

                    Paul P. Langley

SEASON'S TREASURES

There's a season for beginnings
When the world is fresh and new,
When we shape our dreams
Of all the things
We plan and hope to do;
A season for maturing
When we think and work and grow;
And a season for the harvesting
Of all we've come to know.
And each successive season
Grows still richer than the last
As treasures of the present
Add to memories of the past.

                    Mary Saracino

CALL IT LOVE

I pandered my many selves
          away
and called it love.

I hid under the cellophane of
          marriage
and called it love.

Now I want my battered
          heart
in all your tomorrows.

You are the very breath
          of me
that calls your name
          in love.

                    Nell C. Gaither

WHEN ONE OF THEM DIES

The two of them
     Together celebrated life
     For over fifty years.
     Three daughters
     (they had no son to carry on the name)
     One grandchild
     (a girl)
     And three great-grandchildren
     All
     Are companions of a different sort.
     The years ahead look long to
Just one of them.

                    Judy DeVivo

34

UNTITLED

At the interface of summer nights and fall,
Her image at the window gleamed, then waned.
Dark curtain closed a season to recall
When winter's prowess is again ordained

She'd loved like fiction, and denied like truth--
A casual clenched hand betrayed her lie.
She'd found a fantasy born in her youth,
And hung it in the sun to burn and die.

She turned away from summer drenched in ash
That blew into the air with each dark sigh.
Resigned to recreate, she made a cache
For feelings too unwieldly to untie.

    A shadow at the window gives her form
    As she awaits the coming of the storm.

                    Paula Walker

UNTITLED

Spring dew drops fall
from sturdy volleyball net
Attached strongly to spotted windows
my stucco walls provide restricting sidelines.
Glistening sun
calls first play
with morning rays.
Beginning fly ball misses
buzzing into her sticky net
Caught
She smiles
One point for her.

            Jill Purvis

FRIENDSHIP

Before the storm
I stood empty,
with only sorrow
to keep me company.
There was a gathering,
All wanting to share
In my hour of despair.
After the storm.
a rainbow
To brighten my tomorrows.
They had all gone,
But one.
Standing strong and silent
A friend.

                Katherine Wyckoff

MOONPEARL

My unborn child,
You are my moonpearl
You are minister to the earth
The stars,
The eye in the storm,
The wind giver
You are the original
Rain keeper
Shadow watcher
Song maker
You see the world
contained in a globe
A clear sphere
Where forests bloom
Even in the darkness.

                Deborah Hochstettler

JACK-IN-THE-BOX

The Jack-in-the-Box
tenses in the darkness,
holding his coils as close
as possible, awaiting
the painted resurrection
of hat & head -
the inevitable spring
into light.

But what of the boy
holding the toy in his hands,
head bent as if listening -
does something whisper?

Only the rusty hinges
of a metal box.

      Randall Marquardt

la jolla cove

Naked breast, the beautiful blue sea,
rolling and pitching in the surf,
crashing smashing the sea wall:
no place to go. Transfixed,
I looked to the sun's rays glowing
on the water. Frightened,
caught in the whirlpool,
with one mighty sweep I found myself,
arms outflung, face upward tilted, body arched.
The world stopped. I collapsed, fingers dangling,
like a child gently rocked and stroked,
cradled in the sea's vast arms.

      Eugene Rich

SCHOOL DAZE

In the hot stuffiness of the August afternoon,
Shades pulled against the beating sun,
Fans droning in their futile effort
To cool the crowded study hall,
Feet shuffle, pencils drop, heads droop,
Eyes watch the clock...

      Virginia L. Hunt

Syrinx is silent ...   Arethusa sleeps ...
              for Paul Morin

Of this secret remember
the stars still rocking
like threadbare lovers
on polar hillocks ...
novices trying to soften
the blows of their own
skin ...

      Steve Troyanovich

WAITING IS AN OLD WAY

Waiting is an old way
of being discontent
with passing through
a period of something
someone gave you
two sizes too loud,
until you grow
into it or out
of it, to put it in
a closet with the rest
of last year's time.

      Debra Martinez

WHERE TOMORROWS ONCE HAD GROWN

If the world should end today, with you and me
    no more,
Will we spend eternity as in our lives before?
It can't be that much different, though it can-
    not be the same.
Our souls will be the universe, from which our
    love once came.
And we shall share a heaven, no mortal man has
    known,
And there we'll see our yesterdays where
    tomorrows once had grown.

              Cindy Sunshine Walraven

TIME IS PASSING

Fleeting moments ...... Cascade into a swift
Flowing stream -
Time is passing — you live and dream.
Suddenly, youth's spring is winter's old
You ask yourself, "Where did yesterday go?"
Like a wild rolling river, time will not slow.
When life's stream reaches the end,
Will death be time of sorrow or a welcoming
Friend.

              Louise Sharrock

MEMORIES

I found your photo today, resting comfortably among
some old cancelled checks and papers that had long since
lost their importance.
It was nice to see you again.

              Patricia Craven

BROKEN HEART

      My glass heart
tumbles to the dirty sidewalk.
  Sharp broken fragments
    of clear red glass
      cut my feet
      as I walk
    through the jumble.
Tears mix with the glass.
    Cut fingers bleed
  while gathering pieces
with bare shaking hands.
    Screams for help
  penetrate darkness,
a fragile heart lost forever.

              Natalie A. Nalepinski

WINDSWEPT

Dark backed groundswells coil
toward whip weeds,
crashing and smashing upon
rot-gutted shrimpwood.
They break the stars that
get in their way,
tormented, reckless,
driven from the North.

              Christopher A. Strathman

LIFE CYCLE

Conceived in Joy,
Nourished in Hope
Slain in Rancor.

              Roberta Mendel

COMPANIONS

With my companions, the last of their line,
we pass through trails and seek adventure in every leafy path.
We glimpse the hawk in flight and the Monarchs' whispered
exodus into rebirth.

Dreams forge a path where companions, in anticipation,
await my arrival.
Neither time nor dimension invades our passage.
Angels now, they join me in the journey of my dreams.

Carole Frances Confar

WITHOUT YOU

Bittersweet lover who ruled my soul,
You brought me such joy and sadness.
And now that you're gone I'm torn between
Sanity and glorious madness.

D.H. Joyner

WINTER ROSE

So conscious, little rose,
of the thorns that cry your pain.
You fear their sound is all that's visible.
But what of your lavish, pillowing flower
that warm-nestles tired dew,
deep treasures honeyed gold,
and soft whispers fragrant music--
all without a touch of thorn?!
Those spears are only felt by despoilers--
Your lovers, too gladdened by your gifts,
have no fear of thorns.

Jane McConnell

MEMORIES

My treasure's hid in memories
Grown from a vine of grace.
Each small event becomes a rose
Viewed from this distant place.
Life grew so many blossoms
The thorns are hid from view,
And sorrows are forgotten
As I find my grace renewed.
And now I know the secret
Of the peace that blesses age.
In time our grace redoubles
And our deepest sorrows fade.

Dorothy L. Campbell

INDEPENDENCE NIGHT 1980

Blood-red amoeba
multiplying in midair
exploding into colorful bliss,
myriads of pieces.

Jennifer Luckhardt

A HINT OF SILENT PANIC

Modern living makes demands that can ossify the mind,
    With unimportant trivia in an endless daily grind.
It's not the great earth-shaking things which demand our full attention,
    But myriad tiny details, hardly worthy of the mention--

It's the door that sticks, the pen that's dry, and the ever-leaking hose,
    The traffic light that's always red, and the pimple on your nose.
It's your thinning hair, the faucet drip, and the overtime parking ticket,
    That barking dog, taking out the trash, the fence without a picket.

It's the knife that's dull, the clogged-up tub, the pencil with no point,
    The wallet that you left at home, and the rusted plumbing joint.
It's always hustling to keep up without becoming manic,
    And hoping you're not the only one to feel this silent panic.

                    Warren W. Vaché

LONGINGS

Carla says you touch her with the tenderness
of butterflies,
Only I know she longs for eagles.

           Patricia Craven

STARS

The music of the stars
As they twinkle in the sky
Rhapsody for me.

           Helena R. Borgmann

A CONCRETE HAND COVERED WITH TAR

Fingers of civilization grasp the land tight
Till wilderness blood runs brown
Like a dead deer or possum, stiff and smelling.
Painted stripes drip yellow down the middle
To each joint where towns spring like arthritis--swelling and throbbing.
Where each finger ends at the tip of nature
The nail is gradually clipped by vines and trees
And filed by the wind and rain.

           John A. Scarffe

SIGNIFICANCE

Fools give promises - bigger fools demand them!
Am I not my heart within a heart seeking the unknown?
Wounded by a faithless lover's lies...
Searching beyond Life's endless ages -
For some dream that never dies!
My mind, my senses, a moment in madness claimed,
As wisps of fancies strutted back and forth,
Settling down to a shameless apparition of guilt and death!
Upon this deserted plain called Life...
I beseeched a truth of my nature -
It spoke an oath from distant space:
"A star in the blackest of skies,
And the night was an omen of misfortune...
For I was but a flicker in time!"

                    Julian Ocean

YOU'RE SILENT

As
You
Slip
Out
the door

I
I would have liked
To say
Good-bye.

                    Tammy T. Gary

LOVE COMPLETED

                    Love
                I thought
            was primrose praise
            and pinnacled emotion
(joy peaks--symphonic background music)

                    Now
                I think
            pure love was this:
        you held me in your arms
    (all night--you kept the pain away)
    no rhapsody, no heightened glee
                staunch mercy
                wordless you
                and me.

            Caroline Margaret Dunlap

SILHOUETTE AT SUNSET

The rays of the setting sun
Paint a church as day is done;
A peasant plods toward home's soil,
Seeking rest from his day's toil.

Peals of the Angelus bell
Send their sound o'er dale and dell;
The old man stops, bows his head,
Giving thanks for this day's bread.

'Tis silhouette at sunset:
Time to forgive and forget:
Time for thanks before sleep's nod:
Time for prayer to man's one God.

                    Virgil Graber

40

IS TIME FOR REAL?

Timeless months drenched in hurried living sped by
as he ran forever -- from work to school --
    absorbed in self.
As time passed he felt nothing (is joy elusive?)
    but exhaustion, pressure and passive defeat.
Forced inspirations steal away real ones
    as ink lies painfully passive, paper turns parchment.
Why? "There is no time" --
    For what is life's purpose if time is not spent
        and simply passed.
When in the passing of time one gives up his spirit,
    this death can bring to life the flowing ink
        in a frantic search for pad and pen.
Is there realization in a separate peace?

        Kathy Morrone

DON'T GO

April is no time for dying!
A fresh new light is on the hills,
A blooming time for lambs and willows,
The time of birth that overspills.

You who love each tender blossom,
Each blade, each chirp, each sign of life,
You cannot dare retreat from living
While I hang by your thread of life.

My love must be the band that holds you
Here for yet a cherished while.
When amber August burns to ashes
I might accept your final mile.

        Lucile Bogue

YACKITY-YACK

Constant gossip,
Ears a-burning;
Tongue's a-waggin',
Nothing learning!

    Karin Jo Cox

IN AUTUMN FIELDS

Asters cling
in the nude field
while I
grasp and clutch
windblown
over Autumn's edge.

    Nancy P. Kenny

THE SILVER THREAD

Shadows on the wall jar
my superficial sleep.
Can I pretend my life
will never end?
So many doors are closed,
and the last one
is closing.
I hang by a silver thread.
Before me is a whirlpool of black
with a beckoning glow
of radiance beyond.
It is the hour at which
nothing more is.
My Maker, my God, my One.

    Martha Peterson

41

EXECUTIVE BLUES

Woke up in asylum apartment, waiting for my jet to come.
Wondering how AT&T was doing.
Strange how I got here; my limo slipped in a grease spot.
Next thing I knew
I was looking at a stew pot
in an alley.
Had breakfast greasy eggs and a glass of water
served by the village potter.
Jet came
Iran
Got in my second wind
asked about my stocks
They said, shut up.
we're taking you back to the slums.

                    Matthew Rogers

UNTITLED

I saw you dance with Don Carlos
Bourbon y Bourbon, your cousin,
In black-trained gown of Spanish lace,
Mantilla and diamonds in your hair.

I saw you also dancing in the tide
Of Cambria's wild shore,
Now overalled and sneakered,
In a cast-off shirt of mine,
From your tresses sun-flecks
Flashing in the air.

Beach bum or princess, this is written
By one who loved you, contrast-smitten:
All life you treated with a flair
And death you ran to meet, still debonaire.

                    Don Sears

HER WORLD

She sits staring
out the window
at the world
she conceived
in a dream.
All is perfect
according to plan.
She doesn't notice
the bars
keeping her out.

                    Joseph L. Cusyk

HARMONY

Two ice cubes
    Fuse
In the warmth of water.

Two notes
    Fuse
In the warmth of music.

Two words
    Fuse
In the warmth of conversation.

Two lives
    Fuse
In the warmth of night.

                    Barbara Milazzo

42

SUMMER GREEN

A green world of scenic beauty,
with golden sunlight and blue skies,
the greens made more beautiful
by the golden sun and blues of the sky.

One stands in awe at the picturesque
landscape outwardly serene, but within
imagination is running wild in trying
to conceive the beauty of this land.

We look deep and long at the greens
and the blues and breathe deeply
the fresh air of fragrant flowers. We
are here. And what joy to be here
on this planet earth experiencing
Summer green so beautiful beyond change.

Virgie McCoy Sammons

WATCH HIM

watch him,
see how he looks at me and smiles fondly.
listen closely to his flowing liquid words.
listen my youth,
and brand these things into yourself--

for I must remember these magic hours with him.
many many years from now,
when I am alone with my old age,
sitting before the fire of these smoldering memories,
they will be all I have to keep me warm.

these thoughts, kept in a dark frozen place in my mind,
will melt and run like salt tears
trickling down my cheeks.

Sharon L. Harris

RENOIR

Out of the earth come
naked women, full-breasted
as sand dunes, gentle flesh
make waves,
water lingers on their bodies
like dancing fingertips.

They are here to stay
beneath the lattices of willow-
ed arms,
three of them
draw   from the river
great sighs of emotion.
The earth will not sit still.

Pamela L. Laskin

RAIN

Falling
like warm sorrow
over a misty night

Extracting wet smells
from the mossy earth
and folded blossoms
that huddle
timidly together
in clandestine gardens

Silver drops
gathering on a window
to hide
the tears

Jon Varga

43

DISSECTIONS OF THE 21st

rusted locks &
   disposables for
      future anthropologic
         classroom dissection
  all that remains

bewilderment befalls eyes
   on crustaceans remains
      images of oceans from ago
  having ended their journey
     in a waterway
        long dried-up

Dennis Share

ONE MORE

death is something I do not want to know
about it is
something I cry about at night and do
not know why I am crying

I fight it
I parade around it with horns
and drums
until I can't hear until
the horns are an infinite scream.

And all that is placed here
is youth. Youth to carry on, marching
one bright yellow banner which says

Tonight is prom night and I
am ready.

Jay Edward Farina

DESOLATE

Again, retreating to my refuge.
The dark; with a glowing candle
And a stick of incense, my soul
Can bear no more.

Words, give way to tears,
Tears that cannot fall, for without
Love, I no longer know myself.
Fears of insanity haunt my mind.

Frantically, I reach out for God,
Yet feel no closeness. I try to fill
The emptiness; only to find,
I'm more desolate than ever.

Linda Jean Schutz

HATTIE

One of those golden days when
the sun touches
even the medicine bottles
with amber,
her room a warm yellow glow.
The sun on yellow walls,
polished tile, crisp sheets,
hurts her eyes, her pale blue eyes,
faded from squinting too much
into the sun.
She turns her head
away,
lives
too far to come when called.

Pat Keenan

PITY THE RICH OLD WOMEN

pity the rich old women
with their rumpled faces
so ignorant while being rich
that they dress up for empty rooms
and amuse themselves by watching
rain drop to the windowsill.
pity rich old women
locked to their drawing room chairs
and servants who wait with
blank expressions
to announce the daily rendezvous
with teacups
watching their madams tarnish
like silver.

Lynn Wade

THE THING DONE WELL

Whatever end the fates have hid,
One smart thing in life I did:
In my life I loved you,
And I did it well.

Mistakes galore I've made.
Regret's my stock in trade.
Not in much do I excel.--
Yet in my life I loved you,
And I did it well.

Now, song and rhyme elude me.
The sorry ones include me,
But this I'm proud to tell:
In my life I loved you,
And I did it well.

Donna D. Elia

AND THEN CAME THE DREAM

The crowds gathered to mourn
The grave
Of the ageless poet.
A flower was dropped into the earth
That contained the painless face
Of the wordman.
In life he was a pirate,
Reckless and unlawful.
In death he was a prophet,
Philosophical and peaceful.
All that remains is the teachings
Of endless visions and sleepless
Nights.

Robert J. Savino

IN YOUR ARMS ETERNITY EMERGES

Passing from twilight into dawn,
Instantaneous your glance
Cancels blackness in between,
Flowing from light to light,
Darkness dawns an immediate
Succession of rising suns

In your arms eternity emerges,
Flying on wings of timeless time,
Intermeshing spirit on spirit,
While you hold your lips on mine

Trembling, trembled past into flight,
Touching, touched moving into your gaze,
I try to sustain my hold on life,
Together we fall to the skies

Joyce M. Summers

45

HOPE
(To Elizabeth In March)

Today you told me winter wearied you
   And you had begged a momentary rain --
You hadn't even wanted sun, you knew
   That if there fell bright water, there'd be spring
Defeating fat, obscene flakes growing black
   Below the dirty, wheeling town . . . or gray
From booted feet and left an oily track
   Along our walk . . . or painted red where clay
And blood and wingtip tell a robin died . . .
   Requiring but an hour of milder wind,
A temporary pledge of warmth, you cried
   Heartbroken when the snow came yet again:
      But, look! In all the whirling, deadly white,
      Your prayer -- your pain -- put <u>rain</u> with snow tonight!

H.K. Yeager

CASTING OFF

Temple built with bricks of light
Floats on a summer sounding, love-anchored.
Cat's cradle bridge to climb
Behind a plump grandmother, across the web and
Up the spiral staircase to the needle's eye.
Rainbow-hugged firefly of deep dusk,
She hovers over the summer sea.
With earth-wisdom she flicks out a line,
Hauls belly dancers in harem pants of gold cloth
Up the elevator into another world.
Dripping, they cast tea leaves on the sand.
The bridge floats free, the evening temple shines.
Release the summer's sounding,
Let the light ship sail.

Pat Keenan

NEVER JUDGE

The meaning
   Of this poem
In short
   I write
Quite plain
   And simple
Never judge
   A blackhead
By one white
   Or by
Another pimple

Todd D. Wilson

UNTITLED

A vulture-black sky--
Reaching up into it, a tree
   Like spines of coral.

David E. LeCount

A FRIEND

No one knows the start
Nor yet the end
Of the affair.
And yet to exist
Is not to live ...
Without a Friend.

Peter Ritchie, Jr.

TROPHY DENIED

My thoughts drift
> like the boat
> > in languid vein.
> Then . . . splash . . . you leap and twist in pirouette!
A dorsal fin is glistening in the rain.
> The hook inside that cannibal jaw is set.

The line spins out in rage, my fingers burn,
> Cold water boils to froth with bursts of fire.
Fighting with nerves of steel on each return,
> I buckle down to play you till you tire.

At last you slacken pace. My hands still tense,
> I reel the slender thread with hasty pride.
You flex that sinewed tail with impudence,
> As I bring the empty net over the side.

> > Maurice V. Bochicchio

MERCI

I came to you with tearful eyes, my soul was
Torn apart, I had a direction in which to go,
But I didn't know how to start. I remember
You told me to start anywhere, it took me awhile
To begin, I fought a long tough battle and then
I began to win. I know I gave you a struggle
Almost as though you were the enemy, but you still
Stood by me with patience, merci, my friend, merci!
I feel ever so strong now as though I've accomplished
Some great feat, I fought a long tough battle but
I sit in the victory seat. What can I say to you,
Dear friend, you've been so kind to me, I send this
Poem to you with love, merci, my friend, merci!

> > Betty Muschar

SHARE WARMTH

Share
your
kindness,
keep
your
burdens
hidden
A
smile
frees
burdens
within.

> James Terry Foster

UNTITLED

The sound of surf:
on shore a girl practices
her cheerleading.

> Len Rotondaro

UNTITLED

Deep in sunset,
beyond the frozen sea,
sailing starlings...

> Jane Andrew

47

WARRIORS

The seasons are changing us.
What happened to the flower children
Who held up their hands in gestures of love,
And chanted for peace and brotherhood?

This flood of anger has carried them away.
No more peace signs; only clenched fists.
The men are becoming warriors again,
Burning with rage; thirsty for violence.

Provoked, the warriors are rising up
One by one to defend
Land, lives, loves, and pride.
It does no good to wish for peace anymore.

The season has turned.
This is the season of warriors.

Trina Brady

HAND AND CLAY, A CELEBRATION: A RESPONSE

Coarsely ground hands
   mold misshapen clay
   into spun gold.
Thick, undulating muscles
   pound unyielding mud
   into delicate stoneware.
Fiery hot furnaces
   harden soft vessels
   into finished artwork.
All is received
   by enriched audiences,
   or begun again.

Kevin Cornish

CROSSROADS

I am a train station
   lovers, friends and children
pass through me
   on their way
to bigger and better things

                    Yet I remain

You too, you tell me,
   are such an establishment
and know the hollow sound
   of no one
in the waiting room.

                  Shilo Prentice

O GENTLE SEAGULL

Today you are to fly
Your only direction
          to follow the wind
          to fulfill the sky

Take notice of the grass all around
          how it directs only upwards
Pay no mind to the falling leaf
          that is a gift to the earth
You are a gift to the sky

O gentle seagull
Today you are to fly
O gentle seagull
Today you are to soar

bob mullin

SANDALWOOD

Her regal carriage stalks the night-blown sky;
She sweeps white magic starshapes from her path.
Her every gesture mocks most truths on high;
She slays Orion glibly with her wrath.

She passed by me one summer afternoon,
And left a trace of sandalwood behind.
It lingers here and mingles with the rune,
That plays so hauntingly inside my mind.

One springlike eve in autumn she will stride
In out-of-season splendor 'neath the moon
A barely earthbound woman, loosely tied,
She'll float a smile above me in a swoon.

A visionary's vision, night reveals:
A breath of sandalwood both binds and heals.

                    Paula Walker

OUT OF FOCUS

Swallow,
          your image
                    shies away from definition

You are only to be sketched
          to be measured
                    by half-points,
          to be taken
                    by an interior compass

          You direct me through
          a deep, blue woods

               Norma Dillon

CHANGING

The morning tide
has smoothed away
all footprints
of yesterday's passing.
An empty page now,
waiting to record
the countless impressions
of the coming day.
I looked for traces
of my yesterdays
in the patterns there,
but they had washed away
with the force of the waves.

          Bev Fox Roberson

THE RENAISSANCE

Gilded haze forks
Through cliffs,
coats gold
the river below:
a Renaissance,
painting behind rocks
darkly.
Rust-laced trees
silhouette sunward,
heralding Indian
Summer's wind chimes.

Mirrored halo
energizes,
          breathes fresh warmth
          over gray morn.

               Dollyna K. Perry

49

INVESTIGATION

When first the full bright flame of passion stirred
    A selfish inquiry to seek you out,
I left straightway without a parting word
    Or questioning myself for ready doubt.

"Too many loves," I said, "will sit and brood
    When time lays down a dull and heavy hand,
But I shall magnify each fragile mood
    To test the genuine and contraband."

The microscope of mind and matter tried
    But proved no hidden flaw, no telltale line,
Your specimen of love pinned on the slide
    Beside a counterfeit of false design.

So I returned to you, humble and wise,
And read the young dream frozen in your eyes.

        Maurice V. Bochicchio

DANDELION

My days were sighs strung together
on a fragile chain.
Your advent brought an end to the placidity
of life in the blue room,
and with your coming
came the thunder and lightning
illuminating smokey black clouds
that hide in the midnight sky,
as well as bright rock crystals suspended in the void.
We clash and I am a dandelion puff,
frazzled, blown in all directions,
somersaulting on every whim of the wind.

        Maureen O'Toole

COGITO ERGO SUM

Descartes said,
"I think;
therefore, I am."
In my youth
I had never heard
of personal identity
so I was unconcerned
about whether I was
or was not.
Now when I wonder
whether I am,
I think.

        Shirley David

NUMBER ONE

What more,
what less
may come of this....
A mime's missing music
   m=i=s=h=m=o=s=h

restless stirrings
in vacuumless domes

gnomes know

elevation
levitation
relation
relation
relation

        Barbara Burgower

SUNDAY AFTERNOONS

I have known the inexplicable hopelessness
        of Sunday afternoons,
Neatly stacked white linens, black and white cartoons,
Mutilated minds, neatly tucked in beds,
Apple-doll faced, shrinking, balding heads.

Isolation in a cell without bars,
Sparsely filled waiting rooms,
The clinging of metal bedpans,
The unalterable future of one empty bed.

I have seen the spider spin its sticky web
In corner scenarios, over the dead,
Who once watched out of boredom and immobility,
Through sunken grey eyes, pallid white skin,
        of the standard institution.

                    Marilyn J. Barnes

ECHOES IN THE WIND

    Turbulent clouds, fire lightning:
      Coiling through black-monster cracks,
        Hurling fire pillars in the night.
          The earth in mute repose
            Shriveled up and moans.
The sky, blood-red. So many shadows lowering down,
  And turn into human dust shiver in the earth's lap.
    You hear voices descend from the heavens above:
          Like broken twigs crackling
              On the ground
          In the emptiness of sound
            ECHOES IN THE WIND.

                    Lillian Hammer

UNTITLED

A drunken man
looks in mirror,
and sees ocean.

Touching,
  feels cool summer lake.

Fetches baseball bat,
baits teaspoon
with squirming pencil

and settles to fish
for alligators.

                Patricia Rexrode

REJECTION

She struts around
As though she's best.

No one can compare.
A fraud and phoney.

She'll smile and hug you
As she holds the cold
Hard blade.

Beware,
For she'll seek you out.
The fight with her
Will prove nothing.
For she comes in many
Disguises.

                TinaMarie Hubbard

51

LAMENTATION OF AN EMPIRICIST

Within the safe domain of buttressed walls,
I first glimpsed Truth by gentle candle light,
Amidst tall marble statues of the saints.

Bewitched by myths of vast Experience,
I cursed the symbols of my innocence:
The taper's feeble glow; the barren stone.

And now as I ascend a narrow shaft
Toward brazen vistas of metropolis,
Once-sacred icons reappear transformed.

Oh, curse ubiquitous fluorescent lights,
And stone-like faces creased with urban filth,
And give me back the paraffin and flame!

Kathleen M. Thomas

AS DEATH DRAWS NEAR

As death draws near and fashions an embrace
And clings to me as if I were a long-lost child,
I hope with all my heart that those I leave
Will recollect five things of me, if nothing more:
The first is that I always sought to do my share;
The second is that all of those who hated me
Were given understanding, not hatred, in return;
The third is that I loved my love
With all the depth and passion that a man can have;
The fourth is that the turning of my spade may have
    revealed some small fine stone;
The fifth is that I wish no tears to fall as death
    leads me away.

John Bryant

PAINTED POEM

I am a poetic paintbrush
        painting the sky
        in artistic ruin
I am a painted poem
        swimming the ocean
        of loneliness
I am sunsets
        of the earth
        dissolving the ruin
        of loneliness
I am a painted canvas
        of poems washing
        the tears away.

C.J. Cunningham

FOREST LORE

See how stately
the forest stands
as it beckons you
to come and discover
its wisdom
unknown by man.

Jennifer Luckhardt

UNTITLED

March almond-tree
snowing all day long,
the neighbor's steps.

Jane Andrew

EVENING BEFORE A FIFTY-FOURTH BIRTHDAY

Sitting at the kitchen table with my father
An ash tray between us
I smoked one of his Kents
Until it became a butt
Ground against ashes and matches
and unravelled tobacco.

My father's nostrils are red-remains of a cold
And he is drinking Tetley tea from a cup.
I am drinking tea from a mug
The loose leaves flow toward my mouth
with each sip

Music is playing the evening
Background to the deep breathing
Of my father.

          Nancy K. Schwager

FLIGHT

As jeweled sunlight, sweet with joy,
Bends my course, I float away
Inside a brilliant white rose;

Tender hopes are wet with dew.

Crystal pebbles shower me;

I'm scooped out,
Far beyond the petals of dreams;

And thrust into the hollow, sloping calamus
Of separating crimson.

          Dainne Drilock

FOR LOVE

Summer's coins of silver
will buy a shining moon.
Never hoard the gold of sun
unless sands of time have run.
Gold's only spent for love,
and love is gone too soon.

          Patricia McManus

where are the butterflies

when it's cold
and windy
and there are
no flowers

          Joyce A. Chandler

SUN SHOWERS

Sun shower in New Jersey:
where white cloud stands
outside my window, only
To make way for purple
Haze, as rain increases
Its falling

Dog is wet from morning
shower. We are outside
Talking and sitting and it is
Raining on us, wetting
The papers of our cigarettes.

          Fred Chambers

LITTLE GRAY OWL

There's a little gray owl who goes to bed in the pine tree
About the time the sun makes it light enough to see.
He's going to bed when I'm about to rise
For he spends his time in darkness, while I like light in the skies.
Unless I'm out very late at night
I never see him passing in silent flight.
I just hear his who-who-whoos
As his mate he courts and woos.
He spends his day tucked out of sight,
Only leaving the pine tree at dark of night.
When I can't sleep but lie reading in bed
His who-who-whoos echo through my head.
So I consider him an unmet friend
Who keeps me company till night comes to an end.

Pat Hancock

THE SNOWY DAY

Blue-dotted sky
Houses of capped white
****The background to the scene.

Today like most winter days
Held trees of faint pink shadows
With straps of bark embraced.

The bridge over the crystal glazed river
Glossed by smooth-hilled path
Reflecting frail oriental gardens

As the gaze of memories shaded the red brick
And the sheen of summers shone
Norway became distant.

Nannette Dulcie

RICOCHET MEMORIES

As I watch the golden moon
creep over shadowy mountains,
I reflect on the happy moments
with you,
and wish you were here still,
but you are gone.
The moon lures me to gaze
at it again,
shining even brighter now,
its vibrant rays ricocheting
off memories,
of nights just like tonight,
when the moon was full,
and I was happy.

Laura Yon

WELCOME VISITOR

I put on galoshes, my raincoat and hood,
After long months of drought my heart barely withstood,
Gentle raindrops are loosed and I couldn't resist
A walk through the puddles, the drip-dripping mist.

The lilacs and snowballs are bowing in prayer,
There are angle worms sliding around everywhere.
The linden tree's buds wear a young shade of green,
The big naked elm's gray-black trunk is washed clean.

Heavy clouds drop down lower, an inverted dish,
I could taste the pure freshness, a long-nurtured wish.
Gentle raindrops, so rare in our drought-ravaged west,
Won't you change your routine, be a more frequent guest?

                    Margaret L. Schell

THE REWARD OF SILENCE

While the ears must field information
In every inning of conversation,
The tongue should only come to bat
At brief intervals, remember that.

And if you often listen spellbound,
New acquaintances will be easily found.
If with a look only you acknowledge talk,
Then at your praises no one will balk.

It isn't always easy to sit back and nod
When the incessant talker is on the prod;
But when the soliloquy is finally at an end,
You'll find you've made another friend.

                    Frank J. Rubesky

UNTITLED

give me
light verse
there's nothing
much worse
than words
too weighty
even when
I'm eighty
give me
a poem
that skips
from the lips!

                    Kathy J. Waara

MEDITATION

You lay your head
          on my breasts,
While I play with the stalks
Of dead grass
          at my feet

Your dark hair makes
          a splash
Of wounded flowers,
And I who love you
          look far away
                    far away
Where a lost bird
          with wings trembling
Moves silently into the mist...

                    Aline Musyl Marks

55

BIRTHSTONES

Stones of existence
became mine at birth--
Pebbles, jagged rocks,
and heaving boulders jutting
against unsteady horizon...
Smooth roads proved
too alien a path,
and my feet have become
torn and bleeding
from tramping over stony
landscapes in my life.

Ruth Wildes Schuler

THE POOR MAN

Scheming to have
the rich man buys another
and is had.

Yearning to own
the poor man grasps something
and is owned.

Knowing not to
the wise man desires nothing
and has all.

Diana J. Winslow

FALL

The trees stand
tall,
golden stately angels.

Silent, as I gather
fallen halos
from the ground.

Phyllis Yang

SPRING

Iced-lands sizzled
Under atomic rays.
Mountain peaks sighed,
Emerging from sleep.
Iced-water slush
Embraced the naked earth,
Drowning dear life
And seeding birth.

Elizah J. Allen

STEPS

Every step he walks
He walks
Out his life.
The minutes seem slow.
But how fast
A year
A decade
A life
Passes.

Ingrida Zebelins

THE PLEIADES

The heavens so clear
except for the Pleiades
and its tiny stars;
tangled in a silver chain,
will they ever come undone?

Alexis Rotella

HUMBLE SERVANTS

Tall, isolated,
Cacti stand in the desert
Sentinels of hell.

Darrell Fader

REUNION

Your dancing silver teeth have bitten long enough
into cheeks of rose bloom converging with
mountains of mellow weed for tearful wishes of
1970 when I thought I was a man of principle
and everything was as squeaky clean as bathrooms
on a Sunday afternoon when everyone's pattern fits the
white-on-pink laundry room stimulating dreams of
tests and texts for schooldays time shedding innocence
to magical lands missed on days forgotten-then-remembered
and rehashed in dreams and smiles and dead laughter;
reunions and hugshakes and mistakes shaping wrinkles as
depressing as the situation itself.

Jay Edward Farina

SEARCHING

Searching.

But only in my anguish,
Not my present day sphere.
The roving mind, the hoping heart. . .
    The too still feet.

I can still pretend it in my mind
But an imaginary game is never won--
And never lost;
    No matter how you move the pieces.

Perhaps in some different life of the world
You can perceive the thought.

Which of us is waiting?

Linda Aldrich

OUTSIDER

He learned
to live his life
inside a
book
& the woman
became his love
& the children
became his issue
& the old folks
became the parents
he never
had.

Gloria H. Procsal

UNTITLED

raindrops like ghosts
falling through the darkened sky
wings and bridges
ride upon the wind

sitting inside warm
cat eyes gaze
out the window
follow a woman in purple
a puddle
of illusionary desire

my self fills
            the emptiness
her nothingness lends me
                    a smile

Joseph Wollenweber

57

ODE TO AN IDEA

Will I, won't I
What difference does it make
The silent, timeless word hasn't shown
But why does my soul quake?
Through the myriad darkness, gloom and rains that flow
At last a beam; I hear a word
I feel a flower grow.

                    Maurice Shumpert

PHOENIX

O mythical bird,
what perfection
each time,
rising Christ-like
to live six more
centuries.

                    Maureen Doyle

METAMORPHOSIS

        gears

shift

neardawn

untangling

moon

& rolling stars

& the pulling sun

        Kim Myung Soon

INVENTORY

I've got varicose veins now, and receding hair
That's combed to the front to disguise what's not there;
I've got very thick glasses and bad nervous tics;
A nose that's been broken and never been fixed;
A mouth full of plastic, at least on the top;
My car's not exactly the "pick of the crop";
And it's true my wardrobe is nowhere near new;
But I'd be content if I also had you!

                    J. Clancy Brady

TIME PASSAGES

In the stillness of night with memory at hand,
I think of my childhood, playing in the sand;
Not a problem or worry I care to recall,
but happiness & laughter, summer through fall;
As I grew older and put my childhood to bed,
I dreamed of fame & fortune, I'll be important I said;
As I grow older I have learned one great deed,
I am important to me, I am just what I need...........

                    Virginia Gabison

april's gone

farm-fresh skies
gentle breezes
silver rain
sweet flowers
and a timid sun

i'm glad it's may

            Joyce A. Chandler

UNTITLED

I silently cried myself to sleep last night
I wanted to keep my tears inside me
To drown my soul
You see again last night I wanted to die
I wanted death to take me in my sleep
Today I'm not sure why I wanted to die
I just know that if I drown in my silent tears
In my sleep no one will know it was suicide

Marlena C. Daniels

A SMALL CORNER

I want a small corner of this world to plant my
life and watch it grow. I want to feel yesterdays,
watch for tomorrows, while today grows inside me.....

Virginia Gabison

AFTER THE DROUGHT

A caustic web of white lightning
    darts frantically across the sky
Its piercing fingers seek out each corner
    of the apricot-yellow clouds,
And its voice, sharp thunder claps, applauds
    its majesty and heralds the next performance
        of light magic on the backdrop of eerie
            clouds and dusk blue.

Sweet rain on restless leaves creates
    syncopated rhythms with its rustling dance
        of fresh cooling breezes.

And distant sirens shrill, reporting the storm's dangerous fury.

Christiann Dykstra

A DROP

A drop;
That's all that is needed;
To make a plant survive,
To make a life survive,
A drop of rain,
Of sleet,
Of snow,
All the same.

Ingrida Zebelins

SUMMER'S END

the
melting sun
is now high in the
marooned sky,
Birds fly low
over the trees
crying slow
and long.
Michaelmas daisies
line the dejected
garden walls
saying bluntly
we are at
Summer's end.

Diane Turcic

SENSES OF SPRING

Quiet Sunday! Relaxing time!
How we enjoy these freshly blowing April breezes
The trees echo with the melodic strains of singing birds
Each bursting with joyous feeling
And welcoming spring with individual style
My senses are aware and acute
Sweet smells hang heavy in the air
Winter's hibernation has ended
The start of a new life has begun

Karen Coughlin

FOR AESOP

There is nothing a word will not do
to be heard: flatter the mouth, dare foreign
pronunciation, beg involvement with
sensual tongues, promise to whisper the
ear into erection.

But there is more said than should
be. The tongue is a nagging animal, and
if it could not occasionally attract
a fable, it would cleverly taunt the knife to cut it free.

Alan Napier

GRAFFITI

Words of four letters scribbled on a fence,
upon a street, a door, any vacant space;
some so abhor a blankness they fill any vacant place
with drawing, writing, scribbled nonsense;
emptiness is such disgrace.

Kay Bunt

UNTITLED

Leaf
Harbors a circle
Of water,
Strange and smooth
It remains lost
In maple dreams.

Judith Hougen

END OF AN AFFAIR

I brushed back tears
        and tried to hide
My mounting fears
        and wounded pride
As he rushed off,
        serenely cool,
Without my kiss
        to nursery school.

Wanda B. Blaisdell

after the ballet

while you were spinning
I was watching
while you were glowing
I was radiant too

and for a moment
I was you

Jennifer Morris

FISHING

The elapsed fifty years recalled a youthful joy
    of sunning on a homemade raft.
There I held a tree branch rod with a bent pin hook
    attached to package cord, catching fish in their haunt.

When I returned, I gazed at massive brick and stone.
A tar-paved road was where once there was a wooded lane.
Then I beheld dumped refuse in the stagnant stream
    with oil slick floats.
Now all to catch were treadless tires and sardine cans.

                    Morris Kalmus

2/81

I have feelings to share, love to give
But no one to take what I'm giving.

I have time to spend, but no where to go
I'm merely existing, not living.

I have needs to be fulfilled, desires that run deep
But no one to soothe my pain.

I guess I'll lock away my emotions, keep them to myself
Never be hurt again.

                Glenda Anderson-Parker

THE DRAGONFLY

A tiny whirlybird hovering above a turquoise pool,
    slender wings radiating prisms
            in the glowing sunlight.

                Rachel Givan

NIGHT WALK

Walking
on a warm
misty night
the soft fog
embraces me.

Brief lover
who strings
tiny beads
of moisture
on my hair
and eyelashes
tastes sweet
on my tongue.

        Elizabeth Hartman

UNTITLED

Waves weather
us.
Make us cold,
wet.
Two drenched beings
cannot dry
each other.

            Cyndi Hellstrom

DAWN

From gray quietude
comes Sun shining to morn,
Moon fades in her glow.

            E. Leon Hostetler

61

REMEMBRANCE

Our dad has now gone to his rest,
But he left us fond memories and a lesson or two
About living life lovingly; that was one thing he knew.

He knew about airedales and ponies and kids,
He respected God's creatures in all that he did.

Dad's gone, but we know where he is;
God forsakes not his children, of which he was one,
He will reap his reward now, his suffering is done.

I can still hear his "yeah boy", and still see his smile,
Yes, the warmth of his love will be with us awhile.

                    Ron Austin

MR. X

I keep a blank space on my i.d. card
I don't have any initials on my handkerchief
I like to ring doorbells and run away
I am undefined like
A greasestain on a rainslicked sidewalk

All I want to do
Is vegetate under a strong sun
Play dead in a lifeboat
In the middle of the most beautiful lake
Please leave me alone

If I could
I'd stick my finger in this projector screen of life
Even if it hurts

                Reginald L. Friday

BUTTER FLYS

wisp
spring airways
hopping
floating
jumping
winds waves
dying
on the flower
November.

          Richard T. Orlando

living alone

i'm living alone
in the universe

just me my
Self
and some one thousand

fragments

in an old
notebook

everything else
is just an empty shell

in italics

            Jessica Burns

62

LINES ON MY ARTHRITIS

Each morning when I awake and try to rise,
I find crippling arthritis has me in its grasp;
The pain is severe at times and my being cries
As I reach for a doorknob or bureau I can clasp.
The pain eases somewhat as the morning wanes,
And I am thankful I need no wheelchair or bed;
Yet, all the time some stiffness still remains,
And I wonder at the days that lie ahead.
I am past seventy so should really not complain,
I have walked well for all these many years;
God has been good to me and I did attain
Some cherished goals in life despite crosses, fears.
What a blessing, when young, that naught appears
To enlighten us what may beset the twilight years.

                    Robert Preswick

SHADOWS

The shadow leans against the wall, drawing the eye.
The mind works at the puzzle
What is between the walker and the light.
But the body reacts without waiting for slower synapses
To close, and has already run away.

The walker spends a lot of time
Running from shadows
Before any danger has been defined.

Leaving other areas to grapple with
The mights and coulds while walking,
Breathing hard, again towards always
Shadow surrounded light.

                    Jacqueline A. Jones

we have had enough

we have had enough
of winter
but i am afraid
of spring

false promises
of rebirth
into summer
that will only
die again
in autumn

we have had enough
of winter
but at least
it does not lie

                    jani johe webster

AT EVENING

The sun is sinking in the west,
Shades of night are deepening
        Over the weary land.
Across the peaceful lake
        The moon flings
A shimmering golden strand.
        Purple shadows etch
        The water's edge.

                    Frances Lucille Gorman

63

WAITING

It isn't easy loving someone, you know.
I can't afford to lose myself
Inside your rusty armor,
Though perhaps that's what you think you want.

Years from now
I suppose we'll be here,
Still waiting for the bus
While you raise your shield
And I defend my territory
With love.

                    Martina A. Philipp

HEAVENLY WINDS

I was born
        Of the winds that whirl in the wondrous sky.
Now I live
        For a soft and sweet stroke of summer breeze.
May I die
        As the hand of heaven upholds my head.

                    Stephen Whyte

PICNIC TIME

Ants in the garden, ants on the wall---
Let's pack a lunch, get away from it all!
Battle thru traffic, swelter and groan,
Find a cool spot where at last we're alone.
Now we're so happy we sing and we dance!
But----who's here before us? You guessed it--
The ants!

                    Alice Cowan

IN THE PARK

cement gray faces
            walls in place
pine trees in the distance
            living/ breathing
just a thimble sparrow
            preening on a head
a squirrel stops in notice
            and darts away
the sparrow flies as one arm
            lifts to swat it
the statues are giants
            the sparrow lands again
their life is immortal
            compared to his

                    Keith Vlasak

RANDOMICITY

So casually
an egg and sperm unite
a future poet.

                    Kay Bunt

SLEEPLESS NIGHTS

I ache from the late
Of the night before...
I hurt from the work
Of going on more.
I mourn o'er the worn,
Tired weight in my soul,
And I plead for reprieve
From discontent that I know.

                    Nancy Brier Fuchs

64

DARKNESS

Eerie things present themselves
    tho I try to pretend
And forever turn on a teen light
or one of a thousand silver coloured glitters.
Shadows haunt the night and sometimes
    call out with their special message,
Nighttime lingers for an eternity.
Then suddenly it's morning.
            Thank God, I made it.

              Susan Schmidt

MIDNIGHT RENDEZVOUS

I've been cautioned about desires,
and walking on thin ice,
and getting burnt by fires.
I abandoned my trivial rule to resist
in that empty parking lot on the night we kissed.
Now just one look at your face
tempts me to be closer to uncertainty.
Despite want's frightening intensity:
Burn me.

          Nathalie Frances Jahnes

SERPENTS OF SEPTEMBER

September fallen poplar leaves lie
huddled, heaped against cracked concrete curbings
that edge old city streets, move before
the cold wind's thrusting, rustling, hissing
as if unseen serpents slip beneath
their umber tinted mounds.

        E.I.V. von Heitlinger

TWILIGHT WITH THE GODS

Dusk teasingly plays
capricious cat games
casting sinuous shadows
with feline stealth
undulating sensually-
until moonlight
drinks up the shade
and reveals gentle images-
then glistens delicately
on moon-washed flesh.

The night breathes deeply
exhaling magic essence,
transforming me
into the ageless
Goddess of Love.

        Maureen Doyle

WHAT MATTERS LEAST

Strange...the candelabra,
    Bought in Mexico
Amid Christmas hoopla,
    Should not again bestow
Waxing gladness
    With candles flaming.
Instead...tears of sadness
    Appeared proclaiming
Riches sacred,
    A hollow feast,
Where fools are fed
    What matters least.

        Sue Sutton Willbanks

SOUVENIR

Milkweed white of the sky, take me away
Back to the tadpole world of river rafts,
Where the gulls glide lazily over
Tiny beached sand crabs
That carry their homes wherever they journey,
Where every storm harvests a double rainbow
That I keep in my jar of secrets, by my bed.

The brisk summer air, morning dew on Lincoln roses,
Beach party movies, before the darkened day
When death intruded and decided to stay.
I will climb your rusted ladder,
Grabbing your misty edges for retreat
To be taken back when the smell of life was sweet.

Marilyn J. Barnes

SUMMER WALK

A broken fence,
A rotting house,
                              Found
On a summer walk
                              Through
The warm sunshine
                              Down
A lonely dusty path.
                              Found
In a green meadow
                              Filled
With the sounds
Of laughter and love
Of long forgotten lives.

Joseph Edgar Brown

FINALLY

Finally,
After the heat of the day cracks the valley basin open &
Everything dries brown today,
Slowly- A hot sun sinks into the hills of Escondido, dies- &
In its place, rises a shiver of irritation, aggravating
The dryness & the last desert-like gulp for survival.

Cynthia Wolfer

UNTITLED

We are
old wood -
cured,
ready
for the fire.

Cyndi Hellstrom

CATFISH

With whiskers bordering a wide angry face,
He resembles an aborigine of some desolate place.

He's a dandy, you know, in a Southern-style dish,
But a scavenger on his own — the lowly catfish.

Lynn Moore

DAWN

Sun-drenched choir birds
Prance in royal play
Breaking violet silence
Into layered golden rays

Maryann M. Schingo

IN BLOOM

I saw into your eyes
And gazed upon the flower of your intention.
I grew into you like new clothes
And I wore you in warmth.
Your eyes swallowed me
And I gasped for breath from
An airless moment.
Then, I was in you,
Groping about in the darkness,
Flailing my arms about in fear
Of falling.
Well, I fell.
I surrendered to your tender touch
And felt the petal of your flower brush my cheek.

Barry F. Beaumont

SONNET 10

The sun is counting gold he'll give away.
He starts his tightrope walk across the sky,
A giving king who flings the coin of day
To all who come, the innocent or sly.
He'd celebrate his nuptials, Earth his bride,
Resplendent Earth, so redolent with roses
That none would think Heaven so fair beside.
But in September sleep forgetful the Earth dozes
And dreams the lover she could really see
If only she would open up her eyes.
O will she never wake and find the key
That would unleash the end of all our sighs?
Awake, our Earth, enjoy immortal bliss
And seal your king's sweet courting with a kiss.

Dan Wm. Burns

CHANGES TOO

The concrete is hard
And splitting apart,
Where I walked as a child
When the road had no start.
The buttercups grew,
And the bees knew the way
To find all the honey
On a warm summer day.
Now it's fumes from the autos
That roar as they pass,
And the concrete is hard
Where there used to be grass.

Dawn E. Rutter

UNTITLED

My vision in those days
Stirred mountains in motion
My power was innate
Simply used with action
With impulse at my need

I spoke to trees
My ear against the bark
Would hear - hum response
I wondered about stones
A plea reality
There were no sleepy words
Only feelings wakened
Responded emotions

Albert Pertha

ARKTOS

Beneath the stars, past the Baltic Sea
dressed in the skin of a bear
he prowls the night through the endless hours
of the country of work-worn men.
The poisoned spear in his shoulder bleeds a little
but for his freedom he does not fear.

Anne Frolich

WINTER WINDOW

Snow streams softly past my study window.
Hard black earth lies frozen under cold white shrouds.
I think the snow may fall forever,
and Spring will never come to me again.

E.I.V. von Heitlinger

TO THE VICTOR

Two chattering flag-tailed chipmunks fought,
Scattering nuts as each one sought
To claim them all for his own.
Drawn by the din a third scampered in
And carried the nuts away.

Genevieve Johnson

MOTHER NATURE

Fall arrived, birds gone.
Trees shed leaves, grass dies, God sends
Winter's blanket, snow.

Jane Rodger Zimmerman

PLEASE

Would you mind
if we slept apart?

Nothing
personal,
of course

It's just
lately
I've preferred
coldness

Hearts
can only be
chopped
into so many
pieces, you
know.

Jean Sangster

BREEZY AFTERNOON

Breezy afternoon --
carried away by the wind,
the spiders' silk threads;
weather right for ballooning,
air fills with glittering webs.

Alexis Rotella

WIND

The wind is a force
That only says something good
To a sail or kite

Rebecca S. Rossignol

RHYME

Sometimes I get frustrated writing in rhyme.
It never fails that time after time
While searching for words that sound the same,
A part of my mind always seems to go lame.

Joseph M. Pallozzi

CUCKOLD

She made me so happy
So full and filled
So justified
So able to travel
So able to feel
Because she was never there to stop me.

Alexandra Stoll

SHE

Grace falls
in the wrinkles
of her brow...spilling out
through laughing eyes that greet the warmth
of spring.

Ruth Wildes Schuler

THE BUCK DOESN'T STOP HERE

I just can't agree with those folks who complain
That their money won't go anywhere nowadays.
I've never had problems with making mine go
EVERYWHERE; No, my trouble is, mine never STAYS!

J. Clancy Brady

UNTITLED

Scuttling grey squirrel,
Burying summer in autumn
Coffins of frost.

June B. Deaton

FROGS' NIGHT OUT

Rain splashing the night--
Frogs parked in the road--
Bulging eyes gazing at headlights--
Unaware of danger--
Preoccupied
With their flooded dwellings.

Jane McConnell

RED RIVER

The red river runs through my veins
like a Mongoose chasing prey,
it races along
searching for a place to rest,
a place to call home.

Julie L. Stone

JANIS: TEN YEARS GONE

Dry Texas heat
Port Arthur dust
& rusted Mercedes

Cobwebbed feathers
Broken beads &
Scattered pearls

Marvin Minkler

69

JOYLESS VOYAGER

Angst like a tiger's claw
Screeching across the belly of the Venus Di Milo
Vexation of sunlight
Voyagers of the void
Paradise has become a drag
Ever since they let those new interior designers in
Every day I raise my window shade
Look at some of the holocaust
Lower it again
And go back to sleep

Reginald L. Friday

THE WAY IT IS

Life is contradiction.
The double-edged sword of word and deed.
At one moment it is good.
At another it is bad.
Hurry up and get things done.
Slow down and enjoy life.
Achieve mutually exclusive goals.
Accomplish opposing tasks simultaneously.
Say what you mean, but don't mean what you say.
Be everything to everyone.
Contradiction tears the inner self.

Jim Sutphin

FROST

First frost created
Snow-like scenes on God's great world.
Proves He's in command.

Jane Rodger Zimmerman

THE PERFORMING AUDIENCE

Titles of works of art
are often redundancies,
liken unto three halves
of a circle, leaving
little room or no
space for the viewer
to complete the picture.
Much of the creation is
done by the looker as
well as the creator.

Dorothy E. Kloss

UNTITLED

Here we stood-
        underneath this tree
And here we first touched.

But you were whisked away,
        mentioned in the chorus,
Of the recitative of death.

Now I stand-
        dejected and alone,
Telling this tree
        how much I loved you.

Alan Schueler

FALLEN LEAVES

Gathered round the tree
fallen leaves group like mourners
soon dispersed by wind.

Betty Downing

THE AFFAIR

This is the port seen only at night.
The water of lips and salt and legs.
Tongues rise up like whales,
like imperfect mates.

The sound of the earth sighing
turns the ocean with such anger
that fishermen are ashamed of their marriages.

The young girls who sit on the sand
and touch themselves, are also ashamed.
Hands that recently carried one another
are beached by the moon. Half-eaten peaches
wash up with petals and arms.

The world that accepts anything
watches us and stands by the shore to weep.

Laurette Houle Gutierrez

THE RAIN

The rain can make you blind;
Its voluptuous rush
Hushes my vision,
Leaves me impotent and without fear
In a world of flawed waves.

And though I think I must rejoice,
I wish that I could fade now, into its perfect core,
And feel the soft, slow pull
Of heaven's
Gentle
Morphine.

John Terlesky

BARGAINS IN DAYS

My childhood has vanished,
Carefree joy
Gone shimmering past dreams
Of endless play.
Adolescence disappeared
While I hid
Behind a mask of shyness,
Peeking out.
Adulthood--freedom--here
Is all the
Bargain ever hoped for,
Best of all.

Linda Hutton

RUIN

Cold tumbled stones
dark-veined with vines--
a shell
of unremembered feasts,
forgotten wines.
Pass by
the wistful moon;
you come too late,
and I, too soon.

Nancy W. Basham

SPRING

Red rake
brown heaps of leaves
white crocus crowns
in lilac light

Sita Kapadia

COUNTERFEIT LOVE

Woman alone among the blossoms
Silent thoughts for flowers only
Poems are formed in white and ashen
Wishing to be brightly colored
Hair confined in graceful upsweeps
Wanting always to be loosened
To mask the trace of unseen tears
That tell the tale of counterfeit love
Abandoned now and left to die
Memories drift slowly down to earth
And lay at rest with wilted petals
Sorrow's shadowed upon the profile
Of a love that never was

                    Patricia Dean

DISCOVERY

Have none of us ever wished
to capture some long forgotten
memory and find that it lingers
there...just a little out of reach?

We look around and wonder what was it?
Stirring in the periphery of our mind
that pleased us so when we were very young?
Rainbow colors in a world of light and dark.

Perhaps, one lonely rain-soaked night
we stop at a traffic light and see reflected
on the wet pavement the red, amber and green
dance alive and memory floods our mind--
one brief moment the magic of childhood
comes back to us in living color.

                    Shirley Grey Brewer

VAGABOND

Restless soul upon the Earth,
Listless course, temperate worth,
Spent labor for a day's food,
Song and dance to set the mood,
Vagabond meant to roam,
Vagabond bent to home.
Fires to warm the night,
Sight for the farm light.
Traveler o'er the Earth,
Singer of new adventure.
New sights the Earth 'round,
New experience of exotic sound.
Vagabond meant to roam,
Vagabond now bent home.

                    Frederick David Crist

POET LIGHT

to be
a Shakespearean sonnet
in your one act-passion plays
a wildflower
abstract rooted
so concretely by
your wordy demands.

                    Ethel M. Winslow

WINTER MORNING WALK

Winter morning walk...
My plump red hooded jacket
makes cardinal turn twice.

                    Christine Swanberg

NIGHT LIGHTS

After the house retires for the night
and the busy sounds of day die out
I wrap myself within my soul, resisting
the warm blanket of slumber
to enjoy the only time I can be alone with me
to assimilate the remnants of a fragile sanity.

Oftentimes I struggle to prevent the events
of the passing day from closing in on me,
neatly tucking away the cares of today
to make room for creative mental play . . .

Like an unwilling lover, I surrender to sleep
acknowledging the supremacy of day, but
scheming in my dreams to prolong the night.

Ruthie Grant

A ROSE IN THE SNOW

You are a rose in the snow,
the thunderstorm's rainbow;
a cozy fire on a bitter winter night;
to the blinded man the gift of sight.

You are the first breath of spring
that invites the birds to sing;
frost's first refreshing kiss
that colors the trees with bliss;

the daydream reviving a drowsy afternoon.
You are the vigilant light of a radiant moon;
the elegance and innocence of a snow-draped slope,
you are comfort; you are hope.

David C. Schrader

CORNBREAD

Look at the birds -
see what secrets they tell.

I leave cornbread out
for them to eat,
but when I come near,
they flee.

Are you like that?
Why do you flee
when I come near?
Is it me, or
what I have offered?

McGuffy Ann Wisdom

THE ANTS AND ME

I saw a group of ants.
They were carrying a ten milligram
valium to their ant hole.
So goes the fall of antdom.
(And to hell with ambition!)

Fred Chambers

BUFFALO

Bison
Prairie monarchs
Bearded dark thunderclouds
Insignia of yesteryear
Indians' hope.

Rachel Givan

73

... FIND ME, THE GIRL I LEFT BEHIND ME ...

Light, forcing movement,
Instructs the birthing.
Negated miscarriage
Dissolves my protection
Acknowledging life.

Leman to multitudes
Ensconced by none
Embryonic sapien.

Schizophrene suffragette and vassal
Undulating from harbour to freedom
Buttresses rotting and bombed,
Bugle called to activism.
Suffering, celebrating, adult.

Linda Lee Stubbs

A WARNING

Be careful where you walk, my friend;
The world is revolting.
The sidewalks below are cracking,
The birds above are moulting!

Supersonic jets are in the air,
Satellites and rocket ships in outer space.
Don't look up too often -
You might get Skylab in your face!

Please take heed my warning
For you may never know
Which way Three Mile Island's wind
May decide to blow!

Cheryl Hendry

UNTITLED

I built the box from your design;
I even used your tools.
I had the game won on your turf
Until you changed the rules.

Judith M. Wilkinson

UNTITLED

I think I would drift for a while,
Then after a bit
I'd sit
And cry at all
I let pass by.

B. Wayne Zajac

ROOTS

Love is a lily pad treading deep water,
winds and waves are pushing it
rushing it towards the falls;
its life is only as long
as its roots are strong.

Julie L. Stone

UNTITLED

Another night on the wrong end of
too many miles
and too many months.
One extra pillow,
one less coffee cup,
and not enough words
to finish yesterday's letter.

Barbara Klapperich

SHANTUNG SPRING

Spring arrives on slips of rain.
I have my writing things...my lute...
Peonies unfold at April's edge
And lo, my heart is restless to the root.

Whispers. Secrecy. Ear to door
I wait with coiled hair and cheeks of milk.
The time draws near for which my feet
Were furled to lotuses of silk.

I saw him leaning on his hoe
Among the shoots of young bamboo
Brown and muscled as his ox.
The gate goes wide. Will he be you?

                    Arlette Lees Baker

WHEN WE FELL IN LOVE

When you first met me,
    I was wearing brown glasses.
The eyes behind them
    Mirrored my gentle soul,
Filled with waves of affection,
    Rising with poetry
Over the sea of life.
In spite of marine torments,
    My amorous lyrics
Rose upward to you.
Now, after using blue glasses
    For our 20 long years of love,
I return to my youth,
    Wearing a brown frame again!

                    Renée Anne Viosca

TO THE LONELIEST PERSON, I'M HERE

To the loneliest person in the world
    You've got a friend.
If you smile without feeling
And cry without shame,
    Then join me and we'll travel together.
If you feel saddest with someone
And unhappy alone,
    I see you always.
If your heart feels torn
Between screaming with anger
And packing it all away,
    Then this poem is to you;
The loneliest person in the world,
    I'm your friend.

                    Mara W. Cohen

AWAY ALONE

Foreign places, strangers' faces,
Cars roaring in the night.
Empty feeling, zero ceiling -
Dark clouds - no starlight.

Studied tread, whatever led
My heart to bring me here?
Those I've met are friendly yet-
Dare I let them near?

New city, what a pity
I did not stay at home.
Not even I will stop to cry
When I am finally gone.

                    D.H. Joyner

THE GAMBLE

Now if every hill I climb becomes a mountain
and if every road I take is full of holes
if every thought I think just leaves me weary
then it lights a torch that burns inside my soul

Now if every day just brings on more confusion
and if another day the clouds still hide the sun
if another day just shows me I'm still losing
then I'll wish to God that day had not begun

Now if every step I take is just a gamble
I don't think that I shall pass here anymore
for it's a long way from here to where I'm going
but it's a longer way to where I've been before

                    Ron Carlile

SAMSARA

This becoming occurs repeatedly:
Something like a vapor-
Impersonal, but not lifeless-prevails,
Is content in its meandering way
Until, (just why is the mystery),
It is drawn down by some semblance of gravity
By the common means of distillation
From windy ease to iron weight,
Its temporal fate determined:
To glide through granite drapes of days
And years of imposed purpose
Until the stone of it goes to sand again,
And its ruins befit the air again,
To await the next dissipation...

              Sherry Owens-Austin

A BOX FULL OF MEMORIES

Letters
of smeared black ink
fill the tattered box.
Pictures
of us laughing.
We shared our lives
from long distance.
Cards
now wrinkled and bent
out of shape, told me
you missed me.
Now the tattered box sits
alone, filled with
memories of you.

                    Cori Spivak

THE STILLNESS OF NIGHT

In the stillness
    of night
a chill
    snuggled in
frosting the earth
    with a veil
        of white crystals
a wintery trance
    motionless
        except for
the chimneys
    which kissed
        lazy smoke rings
            into the sky.

              Turia L. Knez

76

STAGE PRESENCE

red- twig dogleaf quavers
    beneath the last, shrivelled blossoms

dowdy female pintails
    puddle
        in circles.

maple seeds edge in the marsh, pink- red

and she is still there,
    nose- diving at
    tumbling over
    the shaven park green:
    swallow passing--
    a charismatic flirtation
    in gumbo-clay blues

           Norma Dillon

THE SINNER

Let me pray for the vanity of my crimes. Let me
pay in the coin of my redemption.
Heaven may profit from my guilt.
I have been a poet and a liar.
Let me find a saint to buy my soul.

Mother of Heaven, hold me, eat me
when those who have knelt to pray, are blown away.
Mother, You are the highest bidder
when incense masks the church decay.
For there are moths in the choir, mice in the pews.
I am praying to you in a language I do not
understand. But let me. Let me.

         Wendy P. Basil

NIGHT COMES

On top the lighthouse stands alone
Welcoming all seafarers home
And all is lonely.

Above the heavens dark and vast
In each cloud a shadow cast.
The pool is changing to murky green
The rocks at bottom no longer seen
And all is mystery.

A brooding awaiting twilight
Accepts the coming of the night
Time to stop awhile and think
And feel the day slowly sink
Inside us like a prayer.

         Irene K. Wilson

TO KEVIN

I want it
all -
from the deep fires
burning within myself
I envision a dream
of literary success.
Expressed in the
thoughts conceived
in a literature class
I envision the dream
of art-
However, I also
like to eat.

         Rachel L. Grant

POEM FOR DANIEL

Old pain, velvet, pain formal and contained--
Raggedy sane writer with poems; coffee stained-
First breathless; now restrained.
Now, you're memory, memory
and I'm some Twentieth Century Emily
dressed in black watching the world
mainlining dreams--
Old pain--more comfortable than your terror-
could our computation contain only error?
could we each be less than half and never equaling one?
Or are you really one and I-- I must be none.

Beverly Moore

DAWN OF DEATH

Silently stretching, a pale moon yawns,
And sinks down through the twilight to welcome
                    the infant dawn,
Softly a life slips from earth's silken embrace,
A soul spins toward a new destiny with infinite
                    grace.
Strike swiftly, sweet sword of Death, glistening
                    with unconquerable power,
Evidence of Eternal Truth has been wielded by
                    Thy hand this hour...

Daryle Douglass Carter

MODERNIZED

Mom, Grandma has a new way of doing dishes;
    She washes them in soapy water in her sink
Then rinses them and puts 'em in a drainer
    And her hands get all wrinkly and pink.

Margaret Giles

STARS

From the womb of time
    A cosmic birth
In the domicile
    of galaxies:

Silver asphodels
    to mime
The eyes of lovers
    As they dream

Katrin Imani

DOUBLEDEALING

I dealt your card
reversed in my future.
Your cup inverted
proved to be empty:
no liquid spilled.

I dealt my card
reversed in your future.
My skirt inverted
clung to my legs:
no flesh uncovered.

Marian Ward Cates

UNTITLED

Some people are for keeping,
Some are for leaving,
Some you won't remember,
And a few you'll never forget.

Debra Moore

78

SETTING A LIMIT

Love, like the first soft snowfall, makes us feel
exuberant and alive, delighted to be part of such
a beautiful happening

Yet, too much love confines us, makes it difficult
to move and grow, and brings on feelings of contempt
and boredom

Too much love, you scoff

Yes, just like too much snow

        Sandy Diamond

POEM

Spontaneity's
lost, overlonging--
spend sometime alone
(even in opposition
I complement you). Feel our
breaths mingle (hearts contrapunt).
Need to hold our separateness
(cherish our oneness--
time--for each). Embrace
me now, and teach me
not to lose it them you me right now forever (at love).

        Albert J. Callaway

UNTITLED

In shadowy woods
white birch glow in filtered sunlight,
hold the day longer.

        Joan C. Sauer

UNTITLED

In the park a naked grey
tree argues hollowly
   with the wind.

An old woman feeds
bread to the pigeons
and as she flies away
the birds turn to
stone.

        Phyllis Yang

PURPLING ALONG

My bike shadow lengthens
lengthens into the pale
   of late afternoon
purple sure circles
pulled out along blue asphalt
   oblate like the globe
heels large as I am large
   large as life
I wheel with a sureness
   sure of my shadow

        Emilie Glen

UNTITLED

Over the wave rolls
   the white mist, crawling into
   the safe curves of earth.

        Karen L. Hotchkiss

AUTUMN'S AIR

The day was young and in no way apart
From countless others past in time and mien.
I had no thought but hasten on my way
As nature's pantomime sped by unseen.

What casual breath of one of heaven's sprites,
No end except her private cause extol,
Could cause a passing sentiment subtlety
Persistently and surely prod my soul?

The moment fled but left its brief bequest--
A fleeting, whispering instance of sachet,
By chance when autumn's air and ploughman's share
Conspired to touch my hand with yesterday.

                    Wayne Nelson

THE INVITATION

Share now my joy, on this warm spring day
    Where specks of sails inch upon the horizon
        and blues melt ad infinitum.
Where gulls stroll casually by
    like tourists on a lark
        with never a thought of threat
        to carry them seaward.
Where wavy bands of heat, like misty ghosts
    caress the spotted sands.
Share now my joy, as did our ancestors of old,
    and worship the beauty of nature's sea sirens
    resounding before us.
Meditate with me, this pilgrimage,
    this gift, this joy that is ours!

                 Christopher P. Sanger

I WISH WE COULD SHARE

I wish we could share
    The difference
Between the words we say
    And the thoughts we think.
    To bring them out
    Into the daylight,
To see if we survive them.

                 Joseph Edgar Brown

SPITE

I drew a dagger
            And stabbed the moon
Squealing like a pig
            It fell
Never more to shine
            On lost love's face.

                 Robert D. Williams

CLASS OF HYPOCRITES

In the front rows
        seat mad people
And they laugh at their lies
        trying to idolize
Themselves

Waiting and wondering
        where do they go?
All into institutions
        club dates and bars
Pretending...to be real.

                 Katherine Marsh

MAILLOL'S STATUE: THE RIVER

When first I came and touched her naked arm
and felt the softness of her breast
my skin danced in half-blind dervish whirls
winding like sheets of burning river-sun

Her hands smooth-splayed at water's edge
bear lotus dreams and thighs of shredded
gold-thread, yielding to serrulate night my
fingers press in blood and holiness.

My flesh sharp cut to hers...ribs raw that hold
Picasso's goat, the Burghers and Balzac.
She watches as they act upon my stage
marking with each strut their indelible craft.

                    Laurence Tancredi

BUT NOT TODAY

I'll take your picture from the wall.
I know it's time to put it away
and rid myself of your lingering memory.
Maybe I will, but not today.

It hurts knowing I still love you.
How long can I go on this way,
longing for the times gone by?
Think I'll just stop missing you, but not today.

I've taken the picture from the wall.
My tears give me away.
If I don't do it now I never will.
Put away all that's left of you - but not today.

                    Robert Taylor

UNTITLED

On our bed of irises
in lowered voices we speak
breaking down the barriers
that hold us back in sleep.
Waiting for that moment
when all will be clear
when each will tell the other
what the one wants to hear.

          Candace Gonzalez Shelton

UNTITLED

When the heart gets cold,
The soul frostbitten,
I think of you,
For the warmth I need.

              Jan M. Baldridge

ENLIGHTENMENT

P-s-s-s-s-t!
Grain of sand!
I.....like you,
Am one drop in a sea
of thousands,
Existing in my own space
And accomplishing what I can,
But, alas, I can move
By free will,
While you, my friend,
Must wait
to BE moved.

              Cynthia S. Greene

81

ALMOST SILENCE

My mind is like a quiet lake
Almost silent
A quiescent pool deep and clear
Where thoughts of you like single heartbeats
Disturb the surface
And circle out forever.

Robert D. Williams

UNTITLED

It was
a candle evening.
A white flame flickered in perfection,
lighting a bit of
the large soft fragrance
of unknown.

Melanie Thernstrom

NOTES

A voice calls ever outward
an arbitrary sign of a lost destination
sound searching for a single ear
the vibration awakens
bestial images of our own essence

the journey which we attempt
the call which we must answer
to   go forth and recognize

our glowing illusions
invincible strength melts
stairways of echoes

Joseph Wollenweber

UNTITLED

Now it is autumn;
the red, gold, yellow and brown
of the dying leaves
appear as a painter's work,
begun, but left unfinished.

Susan Ideker

WINTER

Within your eyes are things so frail
That shatter my peace
Like ice falling from the eaves.
Somewhere the silence screams
While I open and close to you,
And snow descends everywhere.

Martina A. Philipp

A VISION OF HELL

The children dance on broken bones.
The old men spit out blood.
The undertaker's business fails,...
The death toll, less then none.
The sun's forever blazing
with a heat that melts the mind.
But dark of night consumes this
heat with vengeance so unkind.
This cold invades the nostrils,
with each breath the lungs are torn.
And every soul held prisoner there
Rues the moment they were born.
And Satan smiles in black delight
at all the torment, pain and fright.

Deana Bade

82

GHOSTS

Pastime spirits crowding present-day spaces,
Lurking in shadows and dusty showcases,
Echoes of laughter, sobs and embraces,
Lingering sighs, haunting old places.

Coupling visions faintly outline old traces
Of sunlit beach days which winter replaces;
Heavily breathe the image of faces
Which time took away but never erases.

Nancy Brier Fuchs

RESTLESS NIGHTS

Nighttime started coming fast,
 I knew the sunlight wouldn't last.
As darkness started settling in,
 My fear was growing from within.
I couldn't sleep, although I tried,
 The blackness wouldn't let me hide.
I prayed that it would not be long,
 'Til Mother Nature sang my song.
At last the dawn came streaming through,
 The sun came out, the skies turned blue.
The dark is gone, the memories stay,
 And now we start another day.

Kari Piske

IN EVENING AIR

In evening air hard corners fade into shadow.
Mountains, trees, and walls disappear
As the edge of sight flows near in slow waves.
Darkness falls, a liquid air dissolving all.

Arend Thomas

CHANCES

Sometimes chances are
funny little things;
If we don't greet them
cordially
When they first
come to call,
It's possible
we could never see them again.

Sharon Barnes

NIGHT LIFE

Shadows
grow in the twilight
as we move
away from ourselves
to a world
where truth
is a lie
and what we know
is growing on the ground
in front of us
till the sun sets
and the largest shadow of all
covers everything.

Lee Walker

UNTITLED

September shore:
here and there along the sand,
scattered stonehenges...

Len Rotondaro

83

CINDY

she said "you should know life is like this-
sections of time cornered in a circle, what you
must do is create an explanation. No room to sit
in idleness around a table, without a goal-
getup getout geton..."
emphasized nicely with a right thrust diving
into her grapefruit.

Anne L. Everett

J'ESPERE

When all is said and done--
What is left to me but hope?
My wounds have been licked.
The agony that seared my soul
has burned into ashes.
Now after I have stood
and sifted the dust,
After I have held the black shards
of shattered dreams; The dreams I had
stir within me.
Hope, tenuous as columbine,
causes me to go on.

Mary Louise Tulloss

GREEN GRASS OF WYOMING

The green grass of Wyoming waved to me
As I drove blindly by and caught my eye
Just long enough that I might halt and see
That here was more than pasturage. There by
That asphalt ribbon lay life full and free,
Untrammeled, my own dearth to fructify.

Robert M. Cook

MOSAIC

Man and Luxor fading
to dust
jungle weed
sand dunes
swamping seas.
Nature recants Her own.

Roberta Mendel

FOR SALE ONLY

an old house
i am used and left Behind
empty and forlorn
windows shuttered
wishing one would stay to live
be Comfortable
Happy
tired of seeing the back end of
a moving truck
tired of dust and cobwebs
tired of echoing hallways
and empty rooms
tired of For Rent signs stuck
carelessly in my front lawn.

Marta Livesay

COMETS

I would fling
Comets
Into your night.
Instead,
I'll just sit on my hands.

Judith Berner

PROMISE OF SPRING

Where dry oak leaves shag-rug the ground
   With autumn's rusty hues,
The first wild violets are found
   To chase my winter blues.

When violets bloom and red birds trill the air,
I think of spring and Him who put them there.

Garnet Quiett

WHEN DAYS WERE YOUNG

When days were young and so was I
my nights were sound and calm.
The sun arose and set so fast
that half my life is gone.
      Collecting memories on the way
      along a path that seemed to wind
      parallel with yours, my love!
If only once our paths could cross
just for a little while in time.
      Somewhere in the silence leads
      a place where secrets never leave —
      only you and I, my love.

Thomas R. Smith

MONUMENT

The eerie beauty of the swamp willow tree
Thrust up from the depths of the earth
Like a hand grasping for the heart of the sky
How many nights has inspiration yielded
From the stars gathered in its crown
And parchment history rolled snug within

Charles Lance Fox

MOLE

Burrowing in the blanket
You are a mole
I am the Earth.

Small animal, in fear
Tunneling for safety
I will protect you.

Paul L. Long

IT IS DAD'S WAY

A lipless laugh
slips through his gaze.
This tells me
what I need to know,
whom I yearn to know.
Even so, the meager profession
burns my ears
with its...slow...silence.
It is quiet now and
I have heard
those eyes
say
those unseen words.

Christopher A. Strathman

WINTER CANDLE

The sun lays orange
across the new fallen snow -
a glowing light, in the grey,
dim evening. A candle
in the heart of Winter.

McGuffy Ann Wisdom

THE UNLEGENDARY TRUTH

As King Arthur once said to his pages,
In discussing historical stages,
"With plague, pox, and the rest,
The ultimate 'quest'
Will be to reach thine own 'middle ages'!"

                    Joan L. Kelly

WHEW-ISH

Perfume's based with a certain scented oil
Borne by one who lives under the building
Burrowed deep in winter under the soil.
Wafted through my opened window that smell
So pungent and raw-essence of civet.

                    Elizabeth Andrews

FIFTH OF MAY

you have gone Out
and buried Our love--

            (deep in the beam of some
             lost star wailing
             in the skyless space
             of no-dreams...)

            or in the roots of a dying Tree

I know
because there is mud
on your hands:

and the darkness of it
has stained me where
you have touched.

            Aline Musyl Marks

DESERTER

Dangling from the end
of a bad dream, you hung
your hope. When Michael
found you I swore his screams
would kill us all.
But there is no life
insurance that the one you love
will stay in his socks,
much less stick to his guns
in the civil-
ized war
between what we call
the world and us.

                    Laurie Rudman

NIGHTMARE

And as I dream
The nights go on . . . empty
And if I sleep
Death might await the dream.

                    Robert J. Savino

FIRST SNOWFALL

Endless lines of soldiers,
Pure and white,
Gliding gracefully
In lacy togs of gossamer
Towards a hard-faced tribunal
Of frigid ground
And bare-faced death.

                    Cheryl Micucci

UNTITLED

Recollections of an ordered past
Peel away the years from memory.
Each pause is a lifetime,
As the worn edges of sensibility
Return only briefly,
In momentary recognition,
Before the last foothold is yielded.

Louis E. Bryan

REMEMBER

That night you had swept back your hair
on one side, exposing an ear
next to which I thought you might wear
a flower? I was wrong: You were

that flower; in your hair you wore
the moon: an opalescent tear,
a match for your eyes; and there, there
with the stars I danced being near.

Bruce Lader

VOID

I wish I could relive
Injury you cannot forgive,
For upon your cause I may survive,
The inscribed brutality of our lives.

Void may redeem my life
But love for you, my debased wife,
Will never yield to the fatal wedge
Which solicits the Annihilating Edge.

Eldon Taylor

IMAGES

The street light sprays whiteness
like a haloed star.
I close my window, and a swastika
embraces my room
from the same lamp.
have we turned our lights and world
inside out?

John L. Kirkhoff

THE CONCH

The conch lay at his feet.
Aunt Emma packed it so
carefully in her valise and toted it
all the way from Coral Bay.
She said it was mystical.
He said it was poppycock.

The ocean roars only
if you want to believe it.

Martha Peterson

RENEWING SONG

What give I to have you mine?
Warmest thoughts are lost with time.
Promises that in their hope did hide,
Without fulfillment, hungered and died;
And shining spheres we touched upon,
In their aura lay melted and gone.
For in the darkness I cannot find
The love that made me blind.

Janice Seaver

puzzlement

one drives a car to work everyday two consumes
plastic enclosed items and enclosed plastic items
three always breakfasts with the morning paper and
four writes correspondence using only one side of
new unused pages

thick woods of a combustible morning furnish a set-
ting for these four to argue the merits and demerits
of returning proximal stream stones procured for a
campfire back to their original location leaving
them as they lay or strewing them amidst silent
flora

jhan hochman

DRACULA'S PROBLEM

There once was a man who came alive at night,
And people who saw him died of fright.
He wore a black cape and had a bad bite,
People who met him never saw daylight.

One night while on the prowl, he met his fate,
His victim was too strong and he realized too
late:
A wooden stake pounded in the chest,
Tends to be more than just a pest.

Terry Scheinoha

UNTITLED

The air that flows by
warm with Spring and sweet with grass--
sand in my sandals

Thelma Murphy

MIDNIGHT WIND

Run over my chest
and carry love away.
Only force like yours
contains purity
innocent of everything
including itself.

I lie and wait,
grow wet with dew.
The thorn survives
the scattered rose.

James Cesarano

MIDWIFE

Unlived dreams are
        like aborted babies.
You have within you
        the seeds of your hope.
Fertilize them.
You are
        Mother
        Father and
Midwife,
Deliver your life.

Judith Berner

UNTITLED

A red rose lies safe,
Sheltered by her leaves from harm,
As a vine protects.

Virginia Hilton

ARRIVAL

As always
The sun still rises
For it never sets!
Just opens doors destined
To feel the struggles reaching
Sky's heights.
Meeting in a feast of fleeting excitement,
It bears fruits of overhead riches
Like majestic oaks leafed in dwarfing summer splendor.
Expected mornings of crystal lights
Not to leave,
Come undaunted as surely as spring follows winter,
Edging toward the touching of sensuous dew.

Joseph A. Baust

WOULD THERE BE TEARS?

Mount Rushmore faces,
Carved in the Black Hills way up high,
Faces of presidents of years gone by.
Washington, Roosevelt, Jefferson and Lincoln,
Looking over the country,
What could they be thinking?

So much has happened over the years,
Would they be smiling,
Or would there be tears?

Dan Dowd

ONE OF THOSE DAYS

Did you ever feel
that you were running the race of life
with your shoestrings tied together?

Jeff Richardson

AMARYLLIS

with the still magic
of a short life
explosive in shades
of red
nothing can surpass
my elegant plant

Clo Weirich

AUTUMN SOLACE

Golden autumn sun,
Caressing amber hills,
Solace ere snow falls.

Florence F. Ickes

WORDS

Words...
Used to be my way,
Safe in their loud numbers,
I gave you many words.
But now there is quality
With you
In simply "being",
And something to be said
In the magic
Of silence.

Lorna Dunkavich

SENRYU #128

Red leaves and green leaves
Are dropping from the same tree.
I'm sure it is fall.

Nicholas

89

EVENING

She gathers the folds of her dark velvet gown
around the low edges of the sun
exposing the ruddy glow of breast in uneven
patches of light.

A slight swish of her skirt rustles silk
stirring smoke from the chimneys of men.
Small white teeth escape from her smile
as full lips linger on a lullaby.

And everywhere she is acknowledged
with incandescent orbs
as the mistress of light,
the mother of dreams.

Carolyn J. Fairweather Hughes

COLOR SO PURE

Because of our friendship,
I've grown from a child to a caring woman.
Mornings, I see a blossom,
green leaves, color so pure, and I stand in awe;
then I plunge into work, busy myself,
get high from a day's creativity;
and after office hours, during the drive home,
as I watch the orange, flame-red oval in the sky
sink peacefully to rest for the evening,
I believe that I have today,
and I know that at last, I, too,
have tasted the sheer beauty of that sunset
with my mind, with my heart,
with every fiber of my soul.

Claire M. Lynch

NATURE IN BALANCE

When birds of prey
do earthward glide,
to sweep the meadow
where unwary reside.

Swift be the sighting,
no breaking of stride.
Curved talons at ready,
shrill screeches of pride.

Fulfilling the ritual,
that faint-hearts deride.
Nature the choreographer,
when two worlds collide.

Judith K. Witherow

SAILBOATS

Sailboats
skirting the sea swells
they appear
like a knife's sharp point
dissecting the ocean
from its depths
silent journey
only
the creaking of masts
and the foaming wake
hint
the simplicity of
Sailboats

Steven B. Rogers

IT'S SAID TO BE

It's said to be..the world is round
Yet, I believe it to be square.
I see broken hearts and all the hurt
From its sharp corners..here and there
I've journeyed to each four corners
There's four true things I've found
If everyone worked together,......
We could smooth those corners ROUND.

Louise Sharrock

WIND WAIL

The wind is an eerie banshee tonight,
Howling defiantly at the moon,
As it gleams down upon the plain,
Listening to the wind's plaintive tune.

Gary A. Scheinoha

WITCH'S DESTRUCTION

Her soul is slipping from her
down the long staff
each time she turns a page
or writes a word in the
spell-locked Sorcery Book.
Her eyes are puffy in her
thin and spotted fading face.
She has an unchosen burden:
simply she ate the berries and lay in the bed,
and they gave her the wand to keep her from harm.
Power betrays her.
She will shoulder the stick for a lifetime--
perhaps beyond.

Georgia Johnston

LIFE OF WINGS

Buzzing flies
  hover near bright light...
Lightning bugs stir in darkness;
Mosquitoes lurk in dampness.

Busy bees
  suck honey
  wherever they please.

Powdery thin colorful butterflies
Flutter through the air
Alighting here and there...
To capture fragrance from the flowers
During the daylight hours.

Betty D. Mercer

SEPTEMBER STORM

Suffused with summer's muggy heat,
The earth laid out upon a sheet
Of arid lassitude in form
Of death, I greet September storm
That it might from its fountains fresh
Renew the spirit and the flesh.

Robert M. Cook

FANTASY

misty haloed peaks
  detached from earth
    urge me
      to ride away
        on Pegasus

Clo Weirich

91

BEFORE THE SPRING

In the deer's coat soft as pollen
Lingers a scent of the woods.

Your curved neck suggests delicacy
As you lie cushioned gently
Among leaves and spotted reed plumes
Hiding secret designs without a trace.

Eyes round as the orb of midnight sky
Watch silver threads of rain
Sprinkle
(Just enough to slicken a doe's tender feet)
On rioting weeds
Around the wormwoods greening.

                    Kim Myung Soon

MARRIED TO AN ALCOHOLIC

It all seems like a bad nightmare,
Now that he's dead from drinking
            that stuff,
Devil in a bottle that raises the
            hair
On end; fighting, screaming despair,
Kick, hate, swear and cuff —
Adultery; merry-go-round of sin-
            ning,
Hopeless, frustrated, broken home;
Promises; still chasing other
            women,
Abuse; hiding bottles; spinning
Confidence into oblivion; fiend
            burning in the bones.

                    June B. Deaton

TRAVEL

I cannot rest from travel,
    As long as there are wings,
Adventures to unravel,
    People, places, things.

My soul is ever longing,
    Searching wide and far,
Looking for belonging,
    Reaching for a star.

                    John Mascazine

UNTITLED

The wintry air stills
Like an icy finger raised
Drawing dormant breath
Only to be melted soon
Into a friend's blooming warmth.

                    Karen L. Hotchkiss

FOOTFALL

Each evening
I measure the distance
between my bed
and your chamber door,
        thirty-two paces all tolled.
If I were to take one step
            each minute,
in less than an hour
I could be in
paradise.

                Listen for my footfall.

                    Barry P. Schmidt

AMBITION

Ambition I hereby set thee free
No need for you to dwell within me
For poets and dreamers have no need
For your bag of goods and hungry greed
Puck, I shall rather choose for my Muse
For ease, Truths before you diffuse
Go now find yourself another student
So I may keep my vanities prudent
Take your tinsel tales of fame and glory
Rest now Gallant Gainsayer, quit my story,
In your absence nestled warm is peace
And unrelenting false labours cease.

Stephanie Simone

DRESSED FOR SUCCESS

Trying on selves like clothes,
Making sure they fit in the right places,
Concealing this and showing that.
Finally looking in the mirror,
Satisfied again to be able to say,
This is me.

Louis E. Bryan

HOSPITALS

Hospitals are places
Where people have jobs
And make strict schedules to keep them
While patients must learn the
                    waiting game.
And so practice patience
Until they get out.

Rose Krevit

AFTERMORN

Lips' soft liaison . . .
Eyes' silences lapse and hearts
From silent sleep redound,
Immutable, les cloches sonnent
Encore--the Sunday paper
Screaming to be read.

Albert J. Callaway

ICY

There's a slight nip in the air,
Here you are without a care,
The ground is frozen hard,
Of all your promises I'm tired,
Maybe it's the season,

Maybe this is the reason,
You always seem to me
To forever be...so icy...?

Alicia J. Muse

FORGOTTEN TOY SOLDIER

The broken toy soldier
lies across the wrinkle-free bed,
disfigured and forgotten.
Oh, how I long to see
the covers lay amiss
and the toy soldier tossed
in childish play.
That cannot be so now,
he sleeps in a slumber
too deep to be awakened.

Nancy Dodrill

HIS BRAGGING AUNT

Jonathan Casey grows in beauty
with each passing day.
He walks everywhere.
He encounters staircases in a single creep.
His fingerprints are legend.
He gladdens our hearts with each toothless grin.

Though he passes through adoring hands and
gives his love with innocence,
deep in my heart I know -
Jonathan's spirit will always be free.

And so the miracle unfolds before us!

Carole Frances Confar

A MOMENT

You take my hand
Preparing to cherish
My nails, knuckles, the shape of my bone
Beyond the view of your glance
Left wordless beneath your language:
The sound of a wave reaching the height
of its tone
Crashing under control,
Once more let go,
A shore left alone.

Nancy K. Schwager

UNTITLED

Cold winter wind:
Three springs worth of snagged kites
Drop from the treetops.

David E. LeCount

MEADOW GRASS

Blades of meadow grass
Brought down by a savage wind
Bent and broken backs

Rebecca S. Rossignol

IMAGES #1

It's the dream
and the reality, fused into
one being,
that is you.

barb e. hobbs

THOUGHTS

Thoughts come tumbling forth
like a waterfall,
Refreshing wherever they fall.
Droplets, crystal clear as dew,
Come forth from me to you.
Splashing forth to refresh a
parched and thirsty soul,
Rejuvenating energy to reach a
long sought goal.

Karen Ann Tucker

WINTER NIGHT

Cold white crystals fall,
silent as dead stars painting
the slumbering earth.

Jean E. Currie

94

DISCOVERED

She feared his eyes.
She feared the priest would know
that under the stars, while the village slept,
her young lover unbuttoned her dress
and warmed her blood.

She feared his eyes.
She feared the priest would shake his head
and say, "No white wedding dress."
And her mother's eyes would close.
And her father's eyes would burn.
And her lover's eyes would unbutton
her dress again.

                    Pat Mora

THE ACCIDENT

Flashing red lights, drizzling rain
Water on pavement mixes crimson stains
White lines outline where a figure has lain
Lines of someone's love lies slain
Cries of anguish, stunned Black pain
People in back, patience drained
Cursing impatiently for one clear lane
On passing, become more aware of the rain

                    David T. Smith

IN YOUR ABSENCE

When you're gone
I'm unpainted redwood boards
Thirsty and split
Warped upward like fingers in prayer.

                    John A. Scarffe

UNTITLED

As the sun rises
    And melts the dew away, dark
    Petals fold their wings.

                    Virginia Hilton

RIVULET

Love should make us soft,
make us clay, almost like
liquid that seeps into every
pore of the human soul.

                    David Monreal

QUESTION

"I come with spring," you write
With careless, flowing ease.
And once it would have been
A breathless wish come true;
But now I hesitate
To watch illusions fall
Beneath the ruthless test
Of excavating dreams.
"I come with spring," For what?
To break my heart again?

                    Jo Starrett Lindsey

AGELESS

In the light that lasts forever
As mountains grow light
The beauty of an aged face
Reflects in morning's sunlit stream

                    Heide U. Greenwald

95

SMOLDERING EMBER

Poor stammering tongue,
Unable to voice trembling ecstasy;
Screams smothered in dry throat.
But I catch, in one brief touch,
Heat of the flame you shield from the world.
That bloating pain you feel is no stranger to me.
I live you for one moment;
Your veiled luster blinds me.
Imagine the fire let loose!
If you would shout in the streets;
If you would lead men.
But you won't.

Godfrey Green

CLOUDS AND THE SUN

This dear sunny shadow,
How often does it fade and fall,
Casting its bright self
Upon my inner wall.

I look at it,
In wonder and mystery,
But before I have a chance to question it,
It runs away into history.

Karen Genetti

ESSENCE

Evening's fabric lures
Earthlings grasp at dawns of hope
Wake to yesterday.

Harry B. Sheftel

LISTEN TO THE SOFT

Beside the river,
many tiny insects speak
in languid voices.

Barbara Pearson

AUTUMN LEAVES

Autumn leaves falling
Haphazardly to the ground,
Dying a slow death.

Cindy L. Woods

UNTITLED

I wait within myself
Time has swept space barren
The flesh room is empty
I gather time's refuse
That which the soul rejects
The sea accepts
And write each awful fact
Into the white blood book
And note the inner edge of rage
Down the last invisible page

Albert Pertha

UNTITLED

Spring in the country;
The same old road, but I am changed
And all is now calm.

Susan Ideker

LATE FOR THE BUS ONE MONDAY
LAST SPRING

Breathe in sunrise
just cleaned by early raindrops
now hung from perilous perches,
waiting to fall on passers-by
like ripe mimosa blossoms
catch you unaware,
dropping on your lens
blurring otherwise perfect vision
you pause to restore original clarity:
discover stars of yellow roses in full thorn--
and fill a moment of your slapdash life.

                    Leslie R. Chaffin

TO A BELOVED FRIEND

With the velvet of your brown eyes,
you watch over my sleep.
As long as the deep brown pools are near,
My leaves and flowers bloom.
But as they dry,
more each spring,
my leaves fall one by one,
until there is nothing but a twig,
and winter all year round.

                    Patricia Rexrode

THE VISITATION

The telephone rings...
A pan clangs in the sink,
Conversation ceases in its chatter,
The poet waits...

                    Arend Thomas

CLOUD SHADOW

Dimmed by cloud shadow
There lies someone's dream.
Broken and torn . . .
Adrift on the stream.
Caught up with the tide,
Driftwood beyond
Questing for happiness.
A lost vagabond.
Shadows veil the horizon
That seekers pursue
Among shattered dreams
That never come true.

                    Virginia West

NIGHT FALL

Moonpools
          and midnight shadows
Crimson windows
          and blue-lit shutters
A choir of crickets
The soft tap-tapping of a passerby
The serenity of nightfall
                    in a small city.

                    Cheryl Townsend

WINTER VAPOUR

Pulled from its warm winter mitten
Rivers of steam stream
From my hot hand held high
To the crisp night air.

                    Wayne L. Assal

97

QUERY

In alien patterns seeking their destiny
An impertinent radiance my mark the genesis
Of a frenzied cycle emerging from the womb
      of a stoic universe.

If the veil of vanity be drawn
And the wings of truth flourish,
Or strident arrogance straddle
A wistful microcosm,

Will the cosmos shrug in phlegmatic indifference?

      Leonard Gorenstein

PAINTING OF A BIRD

Here we see a small painting of a bird
On a large empty canvas.

The empty space gives meaning to the bird
As the bird gives meaning to the empty space.

Like a human and the unknown,
Those who would fly
Must join the emptiness.

      Phil Turchin

LORELEI

Sweet Siren's Song, you sang to me
and drew me from my home.
And now you sing to someone else,
and you and I are done.

      Patricia Craven

JUST A POEM

This poem has no
Depth. I am not try-
Ing to convey a
Message of great in-
Terest. It does not
Have to be unfold-
Ed. There are no se-
Cret stairways or trap-
Doors. It is just a
      Poem.

      Vanessa G. Wright

NIGHT OF SILENCE

There comes a night
of silence: a child
staring at the open
closet door in the
darkened room....
a mother tiptoeing,
covering up her
children....a father's
light breathing....
before he snores.

      Maryetta Kelsick Boose

EARTH ANTENNAE

Spring backyard pose—
slender pines jut forth into midnight
silent earth antennae.

      M. Wad

HAUNTED SCENARIO

Something is lost; something is wrong;
Love is missing; our dreams are gone.
Instead of a satisfied feeling I know
A hungering deep within my soul.

What's happened to what I thought used to be?
Something's off-beat and out-of-key.
My scenario is shaded off-blue.
When I'd now rather say "Good-bye!"...

      Than "Hello" to you.

        Ellen H. Muse

KISS

A stooping shadow from the sky
And she feels a gentle touch upon her shoulder

Wilfully she lifts her face to feel his kiss
So soft, so warm, pressed into her lips

Ah, love, just like the moonbeams
A wind fluttering through leaves,
The convergence of two flowing streams.

        Erich Krueger

UNTITLED

The art of silence
Is like a drop of water
Rolling off a leaf---
That noiseless splash
Making waves and waves.

    Joseph D. Kantor

PEG TOOTH

Withered twinges
Of once-radiant pain
Fill the void
Left by your absence.

      Janice M. Agard

FAITH

There are countless ways
And kinds of worship lore.
Yet for all of this,
I spend my waking days
In search of many more.

      Peter Ritchie, Jr.

WIND SONG

Among wind rushes,
Summer song rises
Plaintiff on a Bach chorale,
Streaming tufts of light
Aglint and stranded
By your hair:
Waves of speckled sound
Bend, glisten through
Eyes' high reeds,
Airy and correct,
Seed bursts of love,
Who float, moistened
Of your heart.

      Gary Lemco

ADAM

   Filled with an urgency
     Standing uneven
       In his
          wonder
      Something
       Stirred.

      Elizabeth Hartman

NOCTURNAL VISITOR

Whose spirit did I hear tonight?
Who calls until it sees my light
Once a year on a cold, cold night.
Which loved one calls until I appear?
It chills me, yet I await the night
The spirit calls,
Then takes sudden flight.
Which loved one summons me
From its tree, from its tree.
They say it is a Great Horned Owl
That pauses on its yearly flight.
But why, why, just for one brief night
Unless to say, I remember you.
I remember you.

        Dorothy E. Colvert

BASEMENT CELEBRATION

I sit unlike Ghandi,
unfasted and fat,
causeless, pausing
at a party underground,
watching lines grow under eyes,
between rumblings of cavernous laughter;
sword and sabre wall ornaments
tremble in their sheaths
to cut the cobwebs,
to be buried again to their hilts,
to slash through the trivia
that consumes our lives,
that fill our tombs with frightening
echoes of emptiness.

        Del Corey

THE KNIGHT -- A LADY'S HERO

The window of the florist shop
Displays an ancient suit of mail
And helmet with a plume on top--
As pictured in a fairy tale--
With roses on a lady's veil.
The flowers say her love is true,
And faithful to the Holy Grail,
Which he was destined to pursue.

The chalice gleams in strong detail.
The cup--not bitter--fills with dew
Of roses, on the thorny trail,
Which he was destined to pursue.

        Eleanor Otto

LOVE'S RAINBOW

Our lives touched briefly
   To share a moment's love
When I found the sunset in
   your eyes, beautiful and serene
I tasted a rainbow on your lips
   full of sensual colours
Our lives touched briefly and
   left sweet memories

        Christina Heraty

SKYLIGHT

   There were times
When I gazed into the sunset
   And like a broken child
      Cried.

        Richard T. Orlando

FRONTIER BATTLE

Zig zag erected stone downtown
Between wide alleys
That lead to rows of brick and stone
Where sounds of breath of newborn
Blend with moanings of the aged.
Here there's life in all its stages
And turf for frontier action
Not sites for racquet courts
And swinging clubs on fairway greens.
Here the shouts and noisy rhythms
Seek a blessing for trapped life
Where strife for every breath
And inch to hold
Still is a frontier battle.

                Morris Kalmus

J.L.

I go there to the graveyard
    Sometimes, on summer days -
I sit beside a tombstone
    In evening's warmest rays -

I look at the inscription
    Engraved into the stone
I feel the tears course down my cheeks
    That's why I go alone -

And too, it's just my moment
    A thing I cannot share
A heart that's long been broken
    Because my darling's there -

                Gerri Benton

CHAPARRAL

A star singed the sky
and mountains rang
clear and empty into the night.
Lightning flashed like starving neon;
pink, then black,
nothing at all.
Sagebrush were the sharp fingers
that scratched at you
for answers to the early bend
of summer.
Night froze high and thin
into layers of snow,
pines were walls around us
as we moved on.

                Donna S. Rutsky

MOON GIVER

He promised me the moon was mine
For as long as I should live.
He promised me a lot of things
That weren't his to give.

He'd make the stars my necklace,
A rainbow for my gown,
He'd pluck the sun from heaven's hold
And fashion it my crown.

I cared not for his promises
Of earth or sky above.
He promised me the moon was mine,
But he never promised love.

                Barbara Deines

CHARLIE

Another dawn slithers into the city
the old soul wakes, reaches for the bottle
that lies beside him in the unknown hallway
holding one last swallow.

He brushes the dirt from his torn brown pants
slowly stands, gripping the wall
He mutters "Damn! What a way to start!"
He turns seventy today.

Jeff Richardson

ENDLESS WAR

The farmer goes out every day,
Pushing himself until day's end,
Fighting a useless, losing war
Against weeds and against time.
He's getting older and it's a losing battle.
But still each day he goes out to wage it,
Because the war never ends.

Gary A. Scheinoha

PROMISE

When last your light shown on my face
And I was lost in the warmth of your touch,
Together we drifted from moon to sun
Indifferent to pain and
The eternal tomorrows that haunt
The sins of our yesterdays.
And still, in the shadow of our past
Looms the promise of our future.

E. Leon Hostetler

A NEW ADDRESS

I'll remember this house,
long after the mail is
re-routed. Another box
of space will seem right
then. But this is where
I blew up my life, sticking
dynamite in my past;
    forwarding myself
    to a new address.

Laurie Rudman

LOVE'S PLEDGE

I'll try to be
soft enough to fit beside you
yet strong enough
to hold you high

Bonnie Riechert

APRIL "FIX"

Stilled youth,
catatonic,
sits with fetus form
in a brisk world.
Eyes wide
as their boundaries,
face, winter-pale,
recalcitrant in the spring sun,
slope-shouldered,
smiling aimlessly
as a roaring breeze
rattles pumpkin poppies.

LaMoyne Nations

NIGHTMARES

I am living them.
Resurrected demons
From my unconscious hell.

No cross can stem the vampire's thirst.
He drinks my blood.
Steps turn into snakes
Darting at my feet
Venom burning in my veins.
I search for home
Down unfamiliar, dark streets.

Though I am cold
My body sleeps in sweat.

                    Arleen   Cohen

VISIT TO GRANDMA'S ATTIC

Amid dust motes in sunlight slants
on a day warm as grandmother love,
a child sits on Japanese silk cushions
        (ancient gifts from uncles
            in a world at war)
rocking her one-eyed teddy bear.
Her song a glass slipper, dancing
revelation of magical maidens
atop mayflowers in midnight meadows.
Fairy tea in Depression glass cups
poured for daydream dolls and toy soldiers,
an interlude from tar paper shacks,
a coal mining heritage and the reality
that dragons and trolls abide beneath beds.

                    Linda Beth Toth

MAN IN THE MOON

You peeked in my window
again last night. Translucent
white with acne craters
distorting your winsome leer.
What do you look for with
those empty mooning eyes? I
feel like a naked beach
under your scrutiny, waiting,
at your convenience, for cover
under the tide.

                    Jami Steiner

MORNING

Emerging morning,
        matin birds tune their voices
                distant church bells chime.

                    Jean E. Currie

HOMBRE

I revel in the crust
of my vision,
for it's rolled from the
hearts of the candle dancers.
Scores of rippling murmurs
scorch my layer, but only
to flourish my vessel of truth.
I wire my own wings
to stroke the wind and
fly my own destiny.
My word may not be heard,
but forever.

                    Samuel J. Bruno

103

OLD MAN

Cackling geese clamor overhead
Vivid orange leaves flutter in the breeze
The ominous black cat arches its
back as its enemy advances.

Father doesn't seem to notice.

Creases and wrinkles compose his face
like the rambling brook weaving among the
rocks. One day soon it will be silent.
Father will be silent.

Yes, old man.

Pat St. Pierre

PARADOX

The ship of state just creaks and groans
And labors while the whole world moans
Beneath the weight of debts and loans
'Neath arguments both pro and con
As to whom has been beset upon
And which precept it's best to don.
The hungry still remain unfed
Their poverty is still unshed
While nations build a great warhead.

Dorothy L. Campbell

SPRING

Perfumed wooded dells
In the young springtime of life,
Heady and fragrant.

Helena R. Borgmann

HUNDREDS OF TIMES

It is almost as though
His name is carved within
My heart and mind,
And that the fingers
Of my whole being
Rush over this inscription
Hundreds of times a day,
Like a blind man reading Braille.

Mari Torgeson

THE HALF-WAY MARK

It's all in the way you look at it.
I'm halfway up or halfway down,
caught in this moment by the camera
of your discerning eye.
But can you judge by looking
how the day will end?
Will earthquake tremor
or sudden burst of sound
force my feet upward
or disturb my balance
that I fall
shattered, discarded,
at your rooted feet?

Alice Mackenzie Swaim

UNITY

A thousand fireflies
twinkling in open fields...rise
to mingle with stars.

Jean E. Currie

104

MASQUERADE

Made-up face with painted tears,
The portrait of a circus clown;
For, seemingly to make us laugh,
He hides behind a painted frown.
But somewhere, 'neath his masked charade,
A sadness drenched with lonely tears
Lies quietly suppressed so not
To blot the laughter from his ears.
Alone, backstage, his heart is wrenched
As simulated teardrops fade,
Betraying every facet of
His long pretended masquerade.

                    Lois J. Funk

i don't know if i know

who or what you are
            as the magic sometimes wanes
                    in the spitting illusion
            at what i've seen of you before
      you crept around
      my very core
            to skillfully keep
                    my heart
            within your wandering
            web of mystery

                    Carolyn Murphy

UNTITLED

The sea breaks on sand
Urgently, hurrying away
From the blowing wind.

      Virginia Hilton

ACCOMPLISHMENTS

I know last night I touched a star
I was surprised
for
I felt no sharpened edges
And the glow did not
                    illuminate the room

Though I knew what I had done
I felt no joy
or
sorrow
So withdrew my hand in passing
To wait to ride the comet's tail

                    Judith E. Hannan

JUST WORDS

Just words
Sounds and syllables
With no meaning
No truth, no lies.

Words that fall
As raindrops from your lips
Convenient and ready
Just the right words

                    Velda A. Hatch

UNTITLED

Summer beating sultry
Requiems of lightning
On ragged wheat fields.

            June B. Deaton

BURSTING

growing to the sun
makes me feel
like bursting.

      Mary Jane Kuzontkoski

AFTERGLOW

This child night the air a clearest cold
the black spindles
of wintering trees   thrust upward
against red to orange to pink
in sediment of light layered up   up
to some darker zenith of blackness
but first the violet   to lightest blue
then bluing in infinite adjustment
to its   final darkening
& in the corner of the good sky
rising   in the corner whitely rising
the moon   its sickle tilted
in a pleasant sidewise smile.

                    Paul M. Hedeen

CUP

I am full to the brim;
I have drunk of life.
Now the thirst I wish to quench
Is for silence:
To quaff the calm waters
Beyond despair,
To hold an empty cup-
To be filled with the void.

            Mary-Elizabeth Epstein

UNTITLED

Tinselling air--
Veronica azures the barleyfields
Beyond the well.

            Jane Andrew

WAITING

I spend most of my time
            waiting
                    for checks
                    for phones
                    for people
                    for love.
Sometimes it gets very heavy
        waiting.

                    Linda Bleser Hunt

TAG

Butterfly shadows;
    one pursuing the other
            through shadow branches.

                    Garry Gay

DISCOVERY

I left the poetry buried deep within,
The colors, moods,
Denying it not because it wasn't good
But because others were better,
Therefore....
Rediscovering it now
I find it special:
Barefoot, corduroy,
Loving dragons and cat-tails and mornings.
Could this be why
I could not accept it before?
It sings to myself
Of me.

                    Diane Heald

106

untitled

dear god's diary, today i melted and raped
and sang and built and shifted and tore
and ground and ran and hunted and hid
and cried and lied and tried and killed
and gave life and now
stand overlooking a choice of two

and dear diary, it depends
on this choice to what ends
are in store for you
to exist or not tomorrow
and i'm weary
we are so many ages here

                    Carolyn Murphy

ME

There is a part of me that hides
Tormenting me to seek and find
To ride the dance of day
To fly the narcissistic night
To find the answers
     and never know why...

                Ray Davis

REED IN THE WIND

The tender reed
bruised by the savage wind
is struggling to hold unto life.
O wind, be gentle
let it survive.
Let it live through another spring.

                Betty Farquhar

STORM DREAMS

Storm clouds moving off;
   a rainbow reaches across
      where the old bridge ends.

              Garry Gay

IF I COULD I WOULD

If I could catch a star
I would give it to you
If I could grant wishes
I would make all yours come true
If I could hold a moonbeam
I would light the night for you
If I could paint the sky
I would paint yours blue

                Vickie Finnie

WINTER SPECTER

A barren willow stands fallow,
arms drooping with the weight
of February lace draped on sprawny limbs,
a somber bride left waiting
in the vestibule.
The nest of twigs and sprigs
lies curled in the crook
of a branch, protected but empty
of the tiny speckled eggs
once nestled in a hollow palm.
The tree stands a thing apart
from the sky and the wind and the rain,
waiting to be born again.

              Maureen O'Toole

A THOUGHT OF HER--RETURNED

Sharing feelings of loneliness
with the black city mirages
Walking down memory lane
I stopped and looked in the restaurant
Where I see us laughing with love
Sharing drinks and ourselves
A silent sigh overcomes me
Only to be broken by a passing car
Street lamps glisten, her eyes
Once shed light in mine
Her warmth, gentle skin,
Velvet lips, slowly approaching mine,
"Sir, can you spare a dime."

                    E.P. Govea

SLOW EARTH TRIP

For Explorer I to get so close to Titan,
Saturn's largest moon, was quite an
                    achievement;
So, how come that my Xmas mail
Took so long on an earthly trail
That my friends all sent cards of
                    bereavement?

                    Joan L. Kelly

RAVENOUS REALITY

Drenched with history,
Time, bloated with today, waits
To eat tomorrow.

          Darrell Fader

SMILES OF SUMMER

Your smile across the table
Sunday morning in the summer
I smile back and make you laugh
Sounds that softly float away

Nothing matters but these mornings
Sounds of summer from the street
We sit and wait across the table
Something soft floats back and forth

I try to hold back time forever
Silence sent through empty space
Will you still smile across the table
As summer shadows start to fall

                    Stephen L. Slavin

A MUSICAL NOTE

   To sit between the G and A
   Or know the tritone pitch
Gives justice to the mind and soul
   But often makes me itch.
Rattling on in diminished style
   With augmented flair and form
   Wondering why the beat is off
When my concerto's really warm.

                    Dianne J. Morrissey

FROSTED GLADE

Forest winter walks,
Blades of glass snap underfoot,
Icy branches gleam.

               Thekla

RIVER GOD

The river forms from the ice
That clings to the tree-clad mountains
Who touch the beclouded sky.
In my boat I rest upon
The flow of this moonlit river.
On its green-jade shores I find
All that I need for this journey:
Plums and bamboo curtains,
Wine and shelter from the storm,
And even companionship
If I should so desire.
I dedicate this poem
To the white-clothed river god.
I will never forget his laughter.

David Michaelson

LAST NIGHT

Last night before you climbed into bed
You kissed me on the cheek,
In the morning, breakfast,
In the afternoon, lunch,
Supper never came,
Stopped by flashing red sirens screaming
In the evening, darkness
Comes slowly crawling on its knees.
You are not here at my side
Snatched rudely away like candy,
I like a baby cry
wishing it were last night.

William Price

CLIMBER

The tallest tree in the universe
Grows inside my mind.
I climb it every day ---
Stepping over limbs
Pulling myself
Over the branches,
Through the leaves,
Higher and higher.
I must never look down again,
Or I might fall.

Trina Brady

HAIKU #16

Whippoorwills return,
Air alive with mating calls;
Summer serenade.

Shirley Anne Gorman

SKY OF BEAUTY

There is beauty all around us
In the morning-glory sky
In the rich tint of the cornfields
And the wild geese flying high
In the petals of a flower
In a swan's unrivaled grace
In the smiles of little children
And in an aged face
There is beauty in the rainbow
And the stars that shine above. . .
There is beauty all around us
When the heart is full of love.

Mary Saracino

A PRIVATE PLAYGROUND

In this place
of sandboxes and monkey-bars
where warned-of strangers never come
I break all rules
and keep the child in me.

Here I will stay
beyond the curfew's ring
then
dawdle from my daydreams
slowly

hand-over-hand.

Regina Murray Brault

TO THE STARS

Chase pegasus dreams.
Even when exhaustion burns your lungs.
Reach
for a wing.
Take a chance,
jump on.
Tame the flying beast.
Then sprint again,
after stronger wings.

Judith Anne McCrary

UNTITLED

There toward tomorrow,
I see today,
trying not to be yesterday...

Denise Katz

SPRING

Vibrant blast of color
As jonquils blend with daffodils
To line the distant horizon.
Backyards filled with children
Sniffing the sweet air of Springtime
While planning summer sand castles.

Cheryl Micucci

NOVICE

Excuse me, if I jostle your soul;
But a soul untouched by others
Cannot grow.
And so
I reach out
With careful touch;
But sometimes, lacking skill,
I bump too much.

Judith M. Wilkinson

THE LAST KITE

The last thing that floated in his eye
Was the kite
And, behind it, in the brief blue sky,
All the sun's light.
And then one sudden portion of a wheel,
So hugely black,
Crashed in, so swiftly he didn't feel
How fell the dark
Or how, orphan and cripple, the kite,
The string grown slack,
Fell back to earth, forgetting light
And the last proud arc.

G. Burce Bunao

PREDESTINED GREEN RETREATS

Lone survivor of strip mining,
Forgotten tree, sway in proxy
Of kinsmen felled.

Reforest the barren hill,
Your seedlings be lofty links to ancestry,
Predestined green retreats.

                    Patsye Carico

UNTITLED

In a chair's scrape on rough floors,
A sigh's drip in Shadow's alleys,
A wind's keen through dry stalks,
Echoes the pierced Eagle's scream
As he crashes against shiny black crags
And thuds on the scraped shore
Of the grumbling, muddy river.

                Joseph D. Kantor

THE LAUNDROMAT

I fold
She stares
I look up
She looks down
It is quiet
The dryers muffle all sound
We don't talk
Yet, our clothes do
For we are holding up before each other
All the secrets of our lives...

                Mary Lou Sanelli

UNTITLED

        Dulcet melodies
Graceful droplets from heaven
        gently kiss the earth

                    Rosemary Siders

WHEN LOVE SINGS

Soft is the music
I have listened to time and again.
Sweet is the lullaby
My soul sings endlessly.
Ever since we met,
My heart sings out,
And sweet is the music--
If only you could hear.

                    Pavla Vrsic

I WRITE A POEM

I write a poem while children die
From forces thrown against the sky
While mothers weep and husbands mourn
            I write a poem!
I write while smoke rears up from waste
Though tears besmirch my grieving face
While horror holds my heart forlorn
            I write a poem!
War's madness I can't understand
The wasteful loss of life and land
To rid of pain my anguished soul
            I write a poem!

                    Nina Doughty

111

DC-10 TO LONDON

Close under heaven's eaves
We sail a smooth dark sea;
Free-ranging spirits trace
Their icy footprints on
The cabin glass.
Inside the glass,
A flight attendant offers
Captive spirits.
I choose a wine, let my attention
Linger over caviar and chocolate torte.

Can it be true that 40,000 feet below
Another ocean rolls?

Hannah Fox

MY CHILDREN

I will name you all tomorrow,
    Children.
Tonight I write my "Sons and Daughters"
    Poems.

I will dress you all tomorrow
Send you out into the world
Prepare to be rejected.

Paul L. Long

FIREFLY

Under moonlit sky
Pausing by swift, clean waters,
A vagrant firefly.

Bruce Langbein

PERVERSITY

Machines have secret inner lives
which baffle wives
of Edison
or anyone
of simple state or kingly place.
Without a trace
of shame or pride,
my vacuum glides
right past the dust curls all about,
with smile seeks out
some rug or coat
to stuff its throat.

Carol Hamilton

RUNNER

In the philosophy of joy
I am a runner
Nearing that first full circle,
Passing the post,
Each moment closer
To the final wire.

Mary-Elizabeth Epstein

BEDTIME

As day dimmed -
Dusk covered the child.
A chorus of crickets created a lullaby.

While the trees bent to brush her hair -
The wind kissed her cheek.
Then blew out the sun and lit the stars.

Susan Masinick

A FAREWELL PARTY

Summer's goldenrod,
   dressed now in champagne fluff,
Escorted by sumac--a flash of scarlet
   parading crimson torches,
Maples scattering confetti
   red, orange and yellow,
Hickories holding high
   their banners of gold,
Oaks waving,
   their brown mittens fluttering,
All saying,
   "Farewell to Summer."

          Erna G. Brown

UNTITLED

Visualize eternity
  equate time and distance
    to zero
      and realize the good
        bearing in mind that which comes
        from evil
    become
      self aware
        and know
          Love.

          Greg Senn

UNTITLED

Deep snow in frost light
makes moons of rhododendrons
music of spheres

        Sita Kapadia

a private protest

eyes
looked tired when they woke
are darker now.
but sacrifice pays well
so she still sits at the piano
before turning off
in a droning memory
when her light
was the only.
singing Dylan with a trained voice
like Caruso blowing in the wind
at bedtime.

          Tom Fate

UNTITLED

  Untaming itself
thunder rocks heaven's doors as
    puddles become streams

        Rosemary Siders

FIRST DAY OF FIFTH GRADE

Once I was kelp floating
    drifting with the tide
    mermaid hair streaming
    a seagull's bride
But I was washed ashore
    when the rat of time nibbled away
    all the days of summer.
Now I am a dandelion
    in a field of daisies.

        Betty Downing

REFLECTIONS ON MR. BUBER

The experience of perception is
Equal to the perception of "experience,"
While the sphere of reality relates
Only to the reality of our sphere:
Then the crisis of our environment
Delimits the dimension of our difference,
And the difference in our dimensions
Destruct the existence of "experience."

Eldon Taylor

AM I THE ONE

I love you now; but would like to climb
with you higher . . .
where will this lead - in our affair?
You reaching out to me to take you along,
or me pulling you when the time is wrong!
I hope this won't happen;
being one with you is simpler -
then being two thinking about me and you!

Patricia Anne Solek

BEAUTY AT BEST

Our trip was worth the travel time
For the trees were beauty, at best
With springtime there, and air so crisp
The leaves glistened like gold

It looked as if we were in heaven
For life was never like that
Trees, leaves and billowing sounds
Filled our hearts with wonder

Charlotte L. Babicky

UNTITLED

I died early
So very nearly
Akin to the start,
With slight prayers intended.
No distant trumpet
Echoing for a weary soul,
Only a cool, gray stone
Will be there to reminisce.

Judith Hougen

SILENT HARBINGER

Spring's first butterfly
Gently wings the warm sunlight,
About its splendor.

Thekla

DRESSING MY FEET IN THE MORNING

I see indian feathers,
    the chiefs, red & white
    coming from the sky

They remind me of summer malts

I was real then,
    like you

I'm simply
    running

back to myself

David J. Patarozzi

114

UNTITLED

An angry ocean
         pounds its accusation
     into a rocky humanity.

Carving all that is righteous
         upon the craggy surface
     making infinite patterns.

         Then it retreats...
taking with it the sins of the shore.

Leaving behind
     fine sands of understanding.

                    Stacey Slaughter

GOODBYE

How can I let you go so easily,
watch you pack and walk out the door?
               No tears, few regrets:
               You turn and wave.
I lock the door, pull the shade,
feeling like a prisoner,
               at last,
               set free.

                    Rae Lannon

MARRIAGE

Cheap and unbending
the Grinch that stole my covers
today is ten years

                    Cathy Sigmund

THE GAME

No sadder fate does there await
Ambition's budding thirst,
Than lies inside the business state
There stands the scholar's hearse.
Chauffeured upon well-traveled roads,
No change allowed on trial,
Pallbearers wearing three-piece robes
Traverse but well-known aisles.
Five years perhaps to forge the chain
That wraps the fertile mind,
He plays the game and bears the shame
Toward compensation's shrine.

                    John T. Gerhardt

HAIKU #64

     Squirrel finds a nut
     After digging through the snow.
     He sits and munches.

                    Nicholas

WHISPERS

       voices of chanting people make
visual the hordes of diseased
     others that have embarked on
          destiny's train. It whistles
               hurdling headlong
          into the asphyxiation of
     countless pilot lights nimbly
          cutting the darkness.
     they ask themselves timidly...
               is this for real

                    Rick Sears

115

WHIPLASH

Plummeting westward,
the world leashed to its eye,
sun crashes in a final flare.

Not satisfied with the salt stain
sucked from my father's lifted hands,
it draws from mine,
whiplashes me
into night.

Be ready. The sun
makes no promises.

Evelyn Corry Appelbee

THE WALLS OF SHIH-PAO-CHAI

Monks doze beneath my garden wall.
Let no breeze stir, no cuckoo wake
September sadness where it sleeps.
Let no mist of memory break.

No letter comes to bear your seal
From ancient ports of jade and tea.
Does summer linger in your eye?
Autumn days have come to me.

Arlette Lees Baker

UNTITLED

The acrobat moon
Shows off, sways on a pine top
To the wind's old tune.

G. Burce Bunao

ENCOMPASSMENT

You were the evening fog
Surrounding silently,
Set fast to fill my night
With deep opacity.
Too long I fled the mist
That followed when I dreamed,
And lingered in the day
Where all was as it seemed.
But now I cheer your twilight—
Dark magic must have won,
When willingly I wander
Through dense oblivion.

Lorna Dunkavich

THE AUTOPSY

A Man once died. The doctors came
And lo! What should they find
But a single thread of poetry
Locked in the dead Man's mind.

They read it once and read it through,
They thought on what it said:
"My body's there, in front of you,
But here I am, not dead."

Randall Jacobs

UNTITLED

Indian summer—
    high in the afternoon sky...
        V of gabbling geese...

Garnet Quiett

FEAR AND FIRE

I fear, if I commune with You,
    You will alter my design,
    Make me walk the narrow line,
And seek, once more, the pure and true.
But is this not what I desire--
    To harmonize with heaven's voice,
    Follow with unshackled choice,
And be consumed by holy fire?
Oh, Lamb of Love, bind my fear
    And blind my insecurity;
    Be, for my debt, a surety
Against hell's ravening profiteer.

        Debra Hopkins Stella

HAVE A CUP

The corning pot coughed up coffee
Through its lip
Dripping down the stove
Seeping into the burner
Flames licking the brew
With a blue tongue
Swelling up
Coffeetizing the kitchen
Transporting me into the Columbian Hills
With Juan Valdez.

        Arleen Cohen

HAIKU #11

Tiny hummingbird,
Silver wings beating the air;
Gathering nectar.

        Shirley Anne Gorman

MISSING YOU

The sea is quiet tonight,
As I sit watching the surface
Gently lapping in muted beats--
Knowing beneath it
The currents are ever shifting--
As my thoughts shift
Always towards you.

        Shirley Grey Brewer

SOPHIE'S DREAM
(remembering S.K.)

In April they dragged the river
for her body
waiting patiently under the ice
for months.
She yielded reluctantly,
still obstinate,
emerging only with the entreaties
of three strong men.
Yellow wildflowers nodded rumors,
raising their heads to see.

        Jon Varga

HANDS OF NATURE

The hands of nature paint
with superior colors
far exceeding the handiwork of man
presenting the image of objects
conceived in his brain
and applied with a brush.

        Elsie Halsey Lacy

117

SUNDAY DRIVE

Faith sits sure behind the wheel
And steers me through the blind curves
With tires gripping tight the pavement slick
Until again the roadway broadens straight
And sunlight hits my face with warmth
And eyes I blink reassured with calm
And watch the passing scenery and forget
The road again.

D. William Buck

TELL ME TRUE

O, God! Give me knowledge and fame
Pour ideas into my mind for life to tame
To live in perfection, to die in glory
To tell this world an untold story
Heaven and hell you create for fear
Tell me true when my end is near
I shall whisper the secret in heaven's ear
Hell awaits me not! My way is clear

Farzana Moon

HONEYSUCKLE

Pale white and yellow droplets
Hang in sweet green caves again
And trail lightly down the roadside
Calling softly to old friends --
Where's the little girl whose dreams danced
With fireflies in June
When a silver tear of nectar
Held more magic than the moon.

Lois Taft Phoebus

FALL TRAGEDY

On the unkempt lawn
One wild icicle radish,
Grown five inches tall.

Winter freeze last night -
The summer's adventurer
Lies limp on the lawn.

Margaret L. Schell

AN IRONIC OBSERVATION

Werewolves and vampires,
From out the dreams
Of frightened children,
Make their nights
Bottomless pits
Filled with countless terrors.
But steadily we grow;
And the nights become
Havens for lovers...,
Rejuvenators for the weary...,
While our days are filled
With werewolves and vampires.

Joseph P. DiMino

THE SHADOW OF DEATH

The devil
    took my body.
He swam through my blood;
    like a snake in water,
        and captured my soul.

John T. Savino

MASK

Seashells reflect the moon in strange ways.
A ballad existing in someone's voice
filters through the air in shadows.
Sinking in the fur-softness of sand,
eyes tight, breathing
centered on the shells.

        There is no return.
And the moon explodes the sky.

             Deborah S. Millman

NEW YEAR'S DAY

We get another chance;
one more chance to lose another year.
How many will be behind us when we die?

Fools will celebrate any occasion,
the bottle being mightier than the heart.
There is no cause or reason;
a year is an endless thing.

             Linda Aldrich

THE FALL FOR LOVE

The May Day's breeze lightly bore
a single blossom
from the swollen Bosom fallen.
____The heavy-laden tree had bent__
and swayed and
           All her blossoms stayed
save One
        Crimson.   Rev. 5:9

             Ida S. Barton

UNTITLED

A tree sways
to music the wind plays
Leaves whistle
catching the tune.
Sweeping branches bow their heads
to the captive audience
that awaits the storm.

             Cori Spivak

THE ONE FACTOR

It is you who has a place
for care to grow
that lays open like a cradle
to caress my inner wounds

It is you whom I will follow
with my own seeds
and a watering glass.

             Mozelle Dayan

TROUBLED RAIN

In the downfall pour of troubled rain
silent
yet still unafraid
though weary
constantly we walk
counting steps that step on time
and leaving half gone days gone by
with tear-stained faith
to chase the facing winds

             Ron Carlile

NOT QUITE STILL LIFE

Old Siamese cat
By a brown and blue curtain
Sunbeams on his tongue
Licking off memories of the night's prowl
Stretching out a stiff leg
To range his tongue along the memory
Of a moonlit, backyard brawl
A good memory
A good ache
He won.

Roberta Ann Collier

EVENING RAIN

The evening silenced
The wind at rest
From blue-grey skies above
Came the tears of dark grey clouds;
Misery-stricken grey clouds.
Were they for my sorrow
Or the freshness of tomorrow?
I didn't know
If hope or flowers would grow.
But the rain-drenched ground stilled
The tears they continually spilled.

Janice Seaver

UNTITLED

The peasant child
clinging to mother's skirt,
lends one hand to the chores.

Len Rotondaro

QUIET, CASSIOPEIA

Valkyrie Brunhilda, watch out!
Brigitte, you've been surpassed -
Eclipsed.
The Goddess of the Moon
Creeps warily into Dawn -
Afraid of the competition.
Je suis arrivée!

Janice M. Agard

DEATHS AND SEPARATIONS

I feel your losses through the distance,
Between us there is simply empty space.
I can touch you only with my words,
They too seem very empty.
Absence creates convexities in time
Spanning shorter when we meet.
Time and distance rendered meaningless
By our attachments.

Isabel Marshall

UNTITLED

It is not the escape from a geographical
location we need to free ourselves from
the everyday drudgeries of living.
It is the escape from the limitations
we put on ourselves.
It is through the introspection of our-
selves and to take flight from that
which is within, it's all there.

Debra Moore

TEARS IN THE SUN

no inference as to their cause
downmycheek
acrossmyear
throughmyhair and
disappear
beyond my existence
farther than the smile they didn't see

a smile without a within
within a sadness
without a name

                    Joyce Randolph

BLACK HOLE HEARTS

Do not think absence makes fonder hearts
It's a hollowness, a void, a black hole
Where heart and soul used to be,
And mankind, as a part of nature,
Abhors a vacuum. Slowly
As eternities pass into moments,
Into days, *ad infinitum*, memories
Are sucked into black heart holes
       Until:
It is as if she died long ago
And the times we had never were.

                    Floyd M. Regan, Jr.

ECLIPSES

Sea swells flood to shore
Rise skyward as they attempt
Flight from gravity

            Harry B. Sheftel

THE PLAYFUL WIND

It whispers through parks
on summer mornings & ruffles
the feathers of cooing pigeons;
moving on, it takes a lost
balloon on a crazy tour of New
York City where it is captured
by the branches of an angry tree.
Joyously, it hastens towards the
open sea & becomes a rollercoaster
for seagulls to ride on.

                    Henry Johnson

UNTITLED

I wish
to move amid the living
intent on giving birth
to form, feeling
as I water ivy and azalea
that the verdant universe
is attentive to the touch
of my watering cup.

a woman soaring:
devoted to bread-crumb communion
with sparrow and dove.

                    Kathy J. Waara

UNTITLED

When cherry blooms fade
And the bamboo dries and rots
Does the sun die too?

                    Rose Marie Roth

SILENCES

We speak in a lyrical synopsis --
Blurts of explained curtsies and bows
A formal recital of tested
melodies and counter harmonies,
Watching the time signatures cleft;
Pound four-four notations
To set rhythms to the rhymeless
Falsetto of our lives.

Ethel M. Winslow

THE LIMITS OF THE SKY

And in the end,
When there is no place left to hide,
We'll ride a cloud,
If one should happen by.
Even time will stop,
To see who dares defy
The written laws of man,
The limits of the sky.

Neal P. Collins

THE FACE OF LOVE

Maybe I want you
        because I can't have you
Then, I can love you
        from the deepest part of my soul
Without committing
        me to you
And never having to face the day
        that you may leave.

Ray Davis

UNTITLED

My time
Is not an hour tomorrow;
It is this minute today.
I cannot stop.
Much remains to be done:
What I dreamed
Must now be seen whole.
To create,
To make something lasting,
To build with these hands,
This is the meaning
And the task this moment bestows.

Mary-Elizabeth Epstein

AFTERMATH

Some years ago you died one death,
I died a hundred more,
For memories still lingered on
As time passed by my door.

I've learned now wounded lives resume,
And seasons, healers are,
Yet ever etched upon my heart
There lies a vivid scar.

Sandy Diamond

FIRST SNOW

All over the town
strange white men appear today
out of children's dreams

Thelma Murphy

WISTERIA

petals float
in the rain-
water caught
in the bird bath
bowl, and stone
statues dance
on the lawn,
as slender
steeples stir
the mist.

  Marian Ward Cates

INSPIRATION

You are
a grain of sand
in an oyster.

You
irritate me
and I produce

Poems
(not pearls).

  Judith M. Wilkinson

RETIRED

time, no more deadlines
no bylines and no headlines
only dawns, skylines

  Cathy Sigmund

SYMBOL OF OUR TIMES

A broken bottle that
sank,
Just along the river
bank,
Iridescent in a diamond
fleck,
Had these words written on
its neck:
          "No deposit
              No return."
So unlike the Grecian Urn.

          David Monreal

for César Vallejo

was it your voice jabbing
me on that midnight bus
in Quito--- or just
another drunk indian
bleeding out the scars
of his existence ...

  Steve Troyanovich

UNTITLED

Rainbow sprinkled grass,
the birds gathered beneath
are bathed in color.

  Joan C. Sauer

bleeding

these are
the withered days
with dreams
grown old
and no words
coming at dusk

while winds
and stars
go on arranging
our thoughts

and leaves fall

bleeding

on the path

  jani johe webster

UNTITLED

So many times
I drift back
to the days
that at times
were so hard.

But from where
I sit now-
they were but
a part of all
that was good.

Candace Gonzalez Shelton

123

HOPE

Yet in my darkest hour
Forth springs a hope
Small and fluttery
A newborn butterfly
With wings tinged grey with sadness
And red with heart.
It flounders uncertainly
In a darkening world
And takes with it the beginning of light
A flickering in a shadow
Seen
Then unseen

Donna Lovett

UNTITLED

You beat them all
The other women of my life
The growing sixteen years with mother
A year or two of mistresses
And sixteen more with her who gave
Me children, adults now, and yours --
All others bested by our twenty years
You won

But where do I find victory?

Don Sears

SNOWFLAKES

Weightless on my hand
small fragments of frozen cloud
melting into tears.

Nancy P. Kenny

UNTITLED

The wheat blades are green
Where the tobacco had grown;
Lowering clouds flee.

Elsie Halsey Lacy

AUTUMN SIGHS

Cricket laughter gone,
Songs of summer die away;
Autumn sighs begin.

Cynthia C. Ripp

I FOLLOWED YOU

I followed you to the sun
But had to retreat
In the face of fire.
I went to war within myself
But wore no armor
To protect my dreams.
Burned and beaten, I fought
To keep wholly myself,
Yet melted into you.

Nancy Barrett

PINES

The tall pines swaying;
They sing their song for me.
I sleep with the music.

Melissa McClellan Ware

ANOTHER WORLD

Another world I used to know
Where seeds of kindness grew;
Where dreams were never doubtful
And hate, one seldom knew.
Where men were all born equal;
Each shared the other's load.
Gray skies were lined with silver
Along a common road.
There, in the world I used to know
Roses bloomed in light
And love dwelled full in every heart
From birth to silent night.

Virginia West

RIDING APART TOGETHER ON THE BUS

We each go our own way
day after day
sitting next to each other
not knowing what to say.

Hello stranger next to me.
Won't you say hello?
I know you know I'm sitting here.
And you know I know you know.

Suzie Blues

INCENSE BUDDHA

There...incense buddha
From your holy headshop nose
hangs a jasmine stick!

Christine Swanberg

UNTITLED

I want to meet you face to face
Why must you always sneak up
on people
Like a snake in the grass
Could it be that you too
are afraid
Death show your face

Marlena C. Daniels

UNTITLED

I am looking into a round glass,
where things are jumbled.
        Magnified is the pain
        that flashes by like
        dirty laundry, in a
        big green machine.
Seeing only what we recognize,
Knowing clearly what we hate.

Denise Katz

LOVE'S REQUEST

Believe in me
so I can believe in myself.

Bonnie Riechert

TINY HEARTS

Tiny hearts...the leaves
of wild partridgeberries--
I put them in a vase.

Christine Swanberg

THE PROSTITUTION OF THE YOUNG ARTIST

With spray paint in hand
I write words on the walls,
Selling lines in the Village;
Prosperity calls.
It's calling me here
To its wrought iron gate
Blocking the path to success.
Still they lock me out,
Leaving me here
With the drunks and the queers,
A poet with no patron
Or nothing left to say.

                    Kevin Richert

INDIA

like a thief in the night
            bellies in the dust
  black swans in the paddies
            babies building the bomb
opium bones
            a frenchman
              wiping butter on his sleeve
  brown faces
              millions of brown faces
like cattle

                    Kent Monroe Jr.

UNTITLED

A day in mid-June;
dog and maple shake themselves
after the shower

            Thelma Murphy

INTERLUDE

I feel upon the evening breeze
A finitude of shallow ease,
And I would stop and watch each star
Speak out in night's vernacular,
A piece repeated with each turn
Of earth, its rhetoric, slow burn,
Smoldering comment from light years
Of silent passage no one hears,
But now I see how bright the song,
I'll signal mine, held in too long.

                    Carol Hamilton

HUNTING SEASON

From oil-on-canvas
Stillness
To explosion of muscular
Energy,
These deer in the road
Ahead of me
Split
The crisp grey of dawn
In frightened, fence-vaulting
Flight.

                    Cynthia C. Ripp

FRAGRANCE

A goldenrod steals
kisses from the setting sun
The fragrance of love.

                    Nancy Dodrill

ACCEPTANCE OF ACTUALITY

Where did the golden days all go,
college campfires burning bright,
the laughter and the carefree years
when most of life was sheer delight?
Dear ones gone and friendships faded,
we're mired in practicality.
Is the now in which we survive
compulsory reality?
The memories swirl and mingle
and remembrance is bittersweet.
Yet, I would not exchange today
for yesterday's untutored street.

                    Patricia McManus

I LAUGH FROM WHERE THE STARS ARE CLEAR

Elegance in motion, you make
My heart a bird,
Winging upward pressed to stratospheric heights,
I laugh from where the stars are clear,
Falling like a feather earthward,
Gathered in your arms,
Again and again

                    Joyce M. Summers

GENERAL WINTER

Tantalizingly,
Winter waits from afar, then
Silently conquers.

          Darrell Fader

UNTITLED

It has occurred to me
    that I might
Reach for the stars;
And that they may
    be shining down on me
    to show the way.
Even if I cannot know
    the distance
I will have to go
Or how long it will take me,
Or what I would be
    if I should get there.

                    Olivia McCormack

NEW SNOW

    I gaze at the snow
    Newly fallen and aglow,
    Muffled and silent.

                Bruce Langbein

THE GALL

    How can you wonder
            if I
        (of all people)
        will be true
    Is it not you
            who hesitates
            to commit
                    beyond words

                    Cheryl Townsend

127

MY SON (Michael David Geimer)

With dimpled cheeks and little toes,
With laughing eyes and button nose,
With coos and chuckles he talks to me,
He's just as precious as can be,
This dear son that God gave me.
Of all his charms I am aware,
But they mustn't blind me to take care,
As I assume a Mother's role,
And guide the future of his soul;
Guide me, O Lord, to reach my goal.

                    Shari Kaye Geimer

FIVE CENTS ON A CAN

Six empty cans of
Budweiser next to
the old typewriter

are gathering dust
while acting as
refundable sentinels

resting on the blank
pages and papers
abandoned on the
writer's desk

in front of the chair
inside the forgotten
room

        Marvin Minkler

MUSTANG ROUND-UP

Steel hoof sparking stone:
ridden against unridden
roped into fury.

                    Leslie R. Chaffin

REVEILLE

Trees don lingerie of green
And host the homing-robin.
The song is sung;
An oversleeping world awakes.

                    Genevieve Johnson

SPRING IS LONG DUE

Self-conscious trees,
Wrapped wretchedly
In middle morning mist;
Their bare buds shivering
In nature's fist.

Middle of April.
Yet, the sun
Has not thrust through
The unwashed winter sky.
Spring is long due--
        And peace.

                    George Knepper

JELLYFISH

Along the shore,
Reflecting,
Silently,
The jellyfish dies.

The wanderer
Does not see
The seeming pool
In his path-
Hops in agonized
Surprise
As the dead
Stings him alive.

                    Jacqueline A. Jones

POEM PENCILLED AT MIDNIGHT

I am hungry, I am tired,
I think of the children I have never sired,
I think of myself as one self-scored,
Replete with this treasure so well self-stored:
    A man in a mist, his own land so dim;
    After all, there he is—it should shine back on him.

A.J. Llewellyn

SALUTATION

TUNNELVISION

Opaque. The grey-stained clouds
hang sad and melancholy;
T here is only one way of
U nderstanding the situation
N ear at hand - I don't
N eed others to
E valuate and give their
L ittle opinions - I'm
V ery convinced that
I have the only
S atisfactory way of
I nterpreting the facts and
O nly my views will be
N ecessary.

Hovering along the blanched horizon
they frown upon the faceless sky;
sagging like the anguished brows
of a wise old man
who has borne the weight
of trepidation
without a single bitter tear.

Mark J. Hollister

Judy Lee

THE FOOLISHNESS OF LIGHT

NIGHTFALL

SNOWFLAKES

do not question
with a stare

Blue-winged night
wafts gently downward
and alights
upon the nadir
of a fading, amber day

Like glowing diamonds
In my hair
Announce that winter
Has arrived
And promise
Cleansing of the air
And time for healing
Of the soul.

the men who stalk
the silent streets
on moonless nights
of deepest sleep
beware
the foolishness of light
empty lonely minds
are maddest in the night

Katrin Imani

Virginia L. Hunt

Robert Monroe Smith

129

the river of our love

our relationship
is like a river.
    constantly moving.
rippling and roaring.
    splashing
        over rocks.
in places,
    calm and peaceful.
        gently flowing.
    everchanging.
        rearranging
its many faces.
    and still
    it flows on.

    Vicki S. Mossman

VALUE OF FRIENDSHIP

At one time I believed
  I had a friend.
To make him happy,
I did all possible,
Hoping he too would
    do the same.
But he could only take,
    never give.
I learned nearly too late
  How wrong I was.
It is easier to find
  a buried treasure
  than a true friend.

    Josephine Buttaci

THE COUNSELOR

Allow me
to reach inside you
to caress
your hidden feelings
no one else
dared to touch.

    E.P. Govea

LONDON

London
a year behind me
as I wander
its dark streets
in my mind
waiting endlessly
in the Tube
cry for a
quick return to
lurking daylight
hoping to figure out
why I dream of
London

    Steven B. Rogers

THUNDERSTORM

Harsh thunder rages
Angrily then, growing tired,
Fades to soft murmurs.

    Cindy L. Woods

TURNING

We spun the top
of giddy hues,
joyful reds and
happy blues;
more slowly now
the swirling curves
of spirals ebbing
tiny nerves--
of red and blue,
of me,
of you.

    Nancy W. Basham

LOOKING DOWN

looking down
the puddle becomes
shadow's
        depth.

    Mary Jane Kuzontkoski

130

BIRD OF PREY

A scimitar's slash
On the curve of the stillness
Between the dust
And the white sun

In effortless strokes
Carves the sky in slow circles
The hawk is a blade
On the wind

     E.M. Solowey

HE AND YOU

I lie in his arms,
make love to you.
You are my heartbeat,
he, my strength;
you live in my mind,
he lies at my side.
He protects me --
I protect him
from my love for you.

   Bev Fox Roberson

SECOND IMPRESSIONS

Weave the dream and the
reality together;
form essential man.

   barb e. hobbs

EMOTIONAL EVOLUTION

It's a classic scenario.

And I marvel still
At the paradox
Of love evolving
To hate...
       to loathing...
To indifference...
         To love.

    Ellen H. Muse

LOVE LESSON #14

A keen-edged sword   (Convincing as the blade
  of Abraham at Isaac's throat)
 is a divining rod in the grip of Solomon:
"I shall slice the infant in two— one half
  for each true mother— and be done with it!"
For him the ruse worked like a pagan charm
But Life is never that easy. (For a moment
  let's not talk poetry; no similes,
   no metaphors)   Neither is Love that easy.
    Put a knife or some sharp threat to it.
    Rave about wisdom & sleight of heart.
    Dare Love beyond sane limits, then wait
long enough: Even God has been known
to turn His back on unrequited love.

    Sal St. John Buttaci

MIGRATION

Round sun
Pale still sky
Swirling black and ivory wings

Storks sail
Silent glide
On the rivers of the wind.

                E.M. Solowey

                    MULATTO

                    Where do you grow
                     In a winter snow
                    When only white flakes
                     flow

                    How do you cling
                      To the frozen extreme
                      Of all absolutes with
                      No in between

                        Todd D. Wilson

                                        DONATELLO DAVIS: 27

                                        after escargot
                                        (you know what)
                                        gildings
                                        an entrance-way
                                        a trance
                                        l'esprit dance
                                        touch a little
                                        bit parts
                                        ornaments

                                            David Vajda

CONTRIBUTORS

LINDA ALDRICH, Michigan - "I enjoy reading science fiction, playing the recorder, and writing poetry, especially haiku. I have appeared in a few anthologies, and hope to one day be an astrologer."

EVELYN CORRY APPELBEE, Texas - Proprietor of "Country Trader Wood Burning Stoves and Fireplaces," corresponding secretary for the local Rusk County Poetry Society; published in *Encore, Ivy Farmer, Modern Maturity,* and others.

RON AUSTIN, Illinois - Firestone Tire & Rubber Company manager; business management instructor; has been published in several anthologies.

SHARON BARNES, North Carolina - From North Carolina A & T State University, she holds a B.A. in speech communication and theater arts. She hopes her philosophical and inspirational poems will "provide a wholesome message to anyone who happens to come across her work."

WENDY P. BASIL, California - New Worlds 1981 Poetry Contest winner.

BARRY F. BEAUMONT, California - Published poems in several anthologies; theater critic, newspaper columnist, and novelist.

WENDY BITTKER, Michigan - Diabetes Education consultant and registered nurse; published poems in *The Poet: Fine Arts Society.*

WANDA B. BLAISDELL, Utah - Widely published freelance writer-poet, composer-lyricist, dramatist-singer and doting grandmother of nine.

SUZIE BLUES, Michigan - Published in *New Voices, The Cypress Review, Up Against the Wall, Mother,* and *Snippets, A Melange of Woman.*

MAURICE V. BOCHICCHIO, Pennsylvania - Freelance writer, advertising/sales consultant. Published in *St. Anthony Messenger, Grade Teacher, Poetry Digest,* and others.

J. CLANCY BRADY, Florida - Previously appeared in *Tracings of the Valiant Soul, Mirrors of the Wistful Dreamer, Reflections of the Inward Silence,* and other anthologies.

ERNA G. BROWN, Virginia - New Worlds 1981 Poetry Contest winner.

SAMUEL J. BRUNO, California - Published in *Eternal Echoes, Earth Rare Art Society,* and other anthologies.

LOUIS E. BRYAN, Washington - A partner in "The Elbow Grease Consortium," a party tending, catering, and homecleaning service; published in *The Poet, The Alura Quarterly,* and *Small Pond Magazine.*

JOHN BRYANT, Pennsylvania - His scholarly efforts include works in relative modal logic, systems philosophy, and education. He founded and directed an innovative extended family program at the Unitarian Society in Philadelphia.

G. BURCE BUNAO, California - Member of the board of editors of *Comment;* former editorial director of *Woman's Home Companion;* author of *The Quiver and the Fear,* a poetry collection.

KAY BUNT, New Jersey - "I am 72 and have loved poetry all my life, and scribbled continuously when...maintaining a home as a single parent allowed. I've been published and I'm pleased and proud."

FRANCO BUONO, New York - Has written poetry and short stories such as "I Cry with You Whoever You Are!"

BARBARA BURGOWER, Texas - Has worked as an English teacher, communications assistant for a cattle association, assistant editor for *Southwest Art*, and currently doing freelance writing and editing.

JESSICA BURNS, New York - Creative writing major at Hunter College; has given readings at the Hunter Gallery and at "The Door" in downtown Manhattan.

KIT CARLSON, Florida - Published in *Ford Times*, *Circle K Magazine*, and *Southern RV*. Also writes for the *Orlando Sentinel-Star*.

MARIAN WARD CATES, Virginia - Recipient of a full fellowship to the graduate writing program at Hollins College in 1978-79.

JAMES CESARANO, New York - A Ph.D. student of English at State University of New York at Binghamton.

LESLIE R. CHAFFIN, Kansas - A senior at Wichita State University who works in the advertising department at Sheplers, Inc.

ROBERTA ANN COLLIER, Published in *Cat Fancy*, *The Waif's Messenger*, *Writer's Digest*, *Cats*, and *All Cats*. (Iowa)

KEVIN CORNISH, California - "An 11th grade student enrolled in a creative writing course."

C.J. CUNNINGHAM, Pennsylvania - Published in *Tiotis*, *A Different Drummer*, *Cedar Shakes*, *Affinities Anthology*, and soon in *Directions* and *Earthwise*.

SHIRLEY DAVID, Pennsylvania - "An Army widow who had the privilege of sharing her late husband's entire military career, raised four sons,...lived in five countries A full-time student at Harrisburg Area Community College.

HAZEL L. DAVIS, Washington - Eighty-year-old winner of five merit certificates for poetry last year; widely published.

MOZELLE DAYAN, New York - Presently working as a waitress near her home in Brooklyn Heights. Originally from Chicago where she studied painting.

JUNE B. DEATON, Virginia - "I write poems for sheer love of 'soul music.' It gets rid of tensions and consoles me when I'm lonely."

KAREN DeGROOT, New York - A fifteen year old high school student, who won second place in a 1980 national short story contest and first place in a local essay competition.

BARBARA DEINES, California - Spent her childhood in Saudi Arabia where her father worked for the Arabian American Oil Company; at present a medical secretary.

JAMES DOWD, Illinois - Author of *Built Like a Bear* and to-be-released *Letters to the Pacific Slope*.

BETTY DOWNING, Washington - New Worlds 1981 Poetry Contest winner.

MAUREEN DOYLE, New Zealand - Poetry published in New Zealand magazines and newspapers, and on radio, *Mirrors of the Wistful Dreamer* (New Worlds); member of New Zealand Women Writers' Society and the New Zealand Penwomen's Club.

DAINNE DRILOCK, New Jersey - Poems have appeared in journals and periodicals.

NANNETTE DULCIE, Michigan - Currently changing career into sales; first poem published.

CHRISTIANN DYKSTRA, Texas - Hopes to become a freelance writer of children's literature.

DONNA D. ELIA, Louisiana - Elementary school librarian, two children, one dog, and one cat, Smoky.

TOM FATE, Iowa - A student at the University of Iowa. Has published poems and short stories.

MARY STICKLEY FEAGANS, Virginia - "My hobbies, interests, and dreams lie in the arts, music, minerals, and astronomy since my youth — in the Outer Space World since Sputnik I in 1957, and in writing since 1967."

VICKIE FINNIE, Kentucky - "I love to not only write poetry but to read and collect it... I hope that my poetry reaches out and touches anyone that reads it."

JAMES TERRY FOSTER, Mississippi - Poems published in *Threshold, Snippets, Our Family, Piedmont Literary Review, New Earth Review*, and others.

HANNAH FOX, Florida - New Worlds 1981 Poetry Contest winner. A former meteorological technician for the National Weather Service, who began writing poetry about three years ago.

NANCY BRIER FUCHS, Texas - "I scream loudly on paper, with pen, and through poetry the loneliness, the stresses and the desires still felt in divorced young people of today; every once in a while, somebody hears me and listens."

NELL C. GAITHER, Ohio - Retired librarian. Has written since childhood. Several poems published in various anthologies.

KAREN GENETTI, Minnesota - A seventeen year old high school student. Although she hasn't yet made any honorable achievements in writing, other than a few published poems, she's working up to it.

DOROTHY CORBETT GENTLEMAN, B.C., Canada - New Worlds 1981 Poetry Contest winner.

LARRY GIARRIZZO, Massachusetts - Considers himself "one of the world's few poet engineers."

RACHEL GIVAN, Arizona - "I am 15 years old... My favorite pastime is reading as I grew up without a TV set."

JOE GLEASON JR., Mississippi - Air Force veteran. Insurance background. Poet and Songwriter. Perfects a modern-day nursery rhyme in the Snooky-Sea series of rhymes for children.

EMILIE GLEN, New York - Her poetry has been published in *The Nation, Folio, Quartet, The Christian Science Monitor*, and in countless journals overseas.

FRANCES LUCILLE GORMAN, Missouri - "My poetry has appeared in nine anthologies, three newspapers, *RAM-The Letter Box, Jean's Journal*, and *Vega**."

SHIRLEY ANNE GORMAN, Missouri - "My poetry has appeared in 22 anthologies, *RAM...*, *Jean's Journal, Vega*, Arulo!*, and two local newspapers. Writing poetry is a wonderful outlet for my pent-up emotions."

VIRGIL GRABER, Ohio - Has had two songs recorded by Nashville's Johnny Dollar.

RUTHIE GRANT, Texas - Employed by a commercial lending office of Chemical New York Corp. A volume of her poetry, *Scattered Moments*, will be released soon.

CYNTHIA S. GREENE, Florida - Published in *Christmas Program Builder*, and is currently writing children's stories for magazines and small picture books.

LAURETTE HOULE GUTIERREZ, Arizona - New Worlds 1981 Poetry Contest winner. Published in *Encore* and *Poem*. Also writes stories and novels.

CAROL HAMILTON, Oklahoma - Widely published, a public school teacher, mother of three, currently working on a third novel.

LILLIAN HAMMER, New York - Published internationally. Her poetry is the reflection of life, space, and time. Her goals — peace and brotherhood.

135

JUDITH E. HANNAN, Texas - New Worlds 1981 Poetry Contest winner. "Poetry is a special challenge because words intrigue me so."

SHARON L. HARRIS, Minnesota - Has published in a few anthologies. Head book-keeper at a bank, amateur photographer, and raiser of horses.

ELIZABETH HARTMAN, New Jersey - Painter; published in *The Rose's Hope Quarterly Magazine*; married; one son who is a painter-sculptor.

PAUL M. HEDEEN, Ohio - Poems forthcoming in *Blue Unicorn*, *Antigonish Review*, *Confrontation*, and other publications. Currently a graduate student.

CHERYL L. HENDERSON, Ohio - New Worlds 1981 Poetry Contest winner.

CYNTHIA HINES, Michigan - New Worlds 1981 Poetry Contest winner. A working member of "Fantasy Factory," a Michigan writers' association.

barb e. hobbs, New Jersey - Edited and wrote for the Brookdale Community College's oral history project; owns and operates a town newsstand.

E. LEON HOSTETLER, Indiana - Interested in archaeology, flint knapping, and scrimshaw. Published in *Connecticut River Review* and *Eternal Echoes* in 1982.

LIBBY HUBBARD, North Carolina - "...inspired to write after contemplating love and the nuclear arms race. I hope to die watching the New World being built."

CAROLYN J. FAIRWEATHER HUGHES, Pennsylvania - A newspaper reporter and magazine writer. Has published in *Forms* and *Cathedral Poets, II*.

VIRGINIA L. HUNT, Indiana - Science teacher. Published in New Worlds, *Capper's New Life*, *Wings*, *World of Poetry*, and others.

KATRIN IMANI, Florida - Published in anthologies, recipient of several Honorable Mention certificates in poetry contests. Has published three volumes of poetry.

RANDALL JACOBS, Oregon - "Thank you for accepting my work! I have never had anything published before this, and I really needed the encouragement."

NATHALIE FRANCES JAHNES, Florida - Her other concerns include music and body building. Currently, she is continuing her study of journalism.

GENEVIEVE JOHNSON, Michigan - Published in New Worlds, The Poetry Society of Michigan, *Wings*, *Erehwon* and *Parnasses*.

HENRY JOHNSON, New York - Published in *Blueline*, *Aim*, *New Kauri*, and *Cosmep Prison Project*.

D.H. JOYNER, Texas - Lives with her husband Jeff and children, Michael and Erin.

MORRIS KALMUS, Pennsylvania - Started writing poetry when illness required him to retire.

SITA KAPADIA, New York - New Worlds 1981 Poetry Contest winner. Professor of English at CUNY. Published in India and America, including New Worlds' *Tracings of the Valiant Soul* and *Visions of the Enchanted Spirit*.

KATHY KEOGH, California - "I am 22 years old with hopes of becoming a successful songwriter."

BARBARA KLAPPERICH, Wisconsin - Published recently in *Small Pond Magazine*, *American Collegiate Anthology* and *Sweetwater Review*. Also appeared in New Worlds *Mirrors of the Wistful Dreamer*.

PHILIP J. KOKINIS, Massachusetts - Studies Literature at local colleges; widely published; also writes stories and newspaper editorials.

ROSE KREVIT, California - A painter who writes poetry as a way of ordering her thoughts.

DIANA KWIATKOWSKI, New York - Has published nore than 200 poems; edited the successful *The Poet Pope* anthology last year.

ELSIE HALSEY LACY, Kentucky - Author of numerous poetry collections; winner of poetry awards; listed in several *Who's Who* directories.

RUTH LAINE, California - Honorable Mention in 1978 Collegiate Poetry Contest sponsored by *The Lyric*.

ALANA LALLY, New Jersey - Physical education and health teacher; has been writing poetry since she was a child, spurred on by her poet father.

RAE LANNON, Nebraska - President of North Platte Writers Guild, who writes poetry for its therapeutic value.

PAMELA L. LASKIN, New York - Published in several small literary magazines. She has recently received her Master's degree in creative writing.

JO STARRETT LINDSEY, New Mexico - Member of the New Mexico Poetry Society and New York Poetry Forum; has published in the *Albuquerque Tribune, Albuquerque Journal,* and others.

PAUL L. LONG, Texas - Computer Operations Supervisor; published in *Vega**, *Gusto, Arulo!, The Poet Pope,* and New Worlds; winner of poetry Honorable Mention awards.

DONNA LOVETT, New York - Seventeen years old; currently living in Rome, Italy with her family; she also plays the clarinet and paints.

JENNIFER LUCKHARDT, Wisconsin - "To write poetry is to live in the spirit." Published in *Poetry Pageant 1980, World Treasury of Great Poems,* and *The Living Church.*

CLAIRE M. LYNCH, New York - Works in public relations; M.A. in English from NYU; published in *The New York Times* and various poetry journals.

ALINE MUSYL MARKS, New Jersey - Former high school teacher of English and art; published in *Poet Lore, Bitterroot, Alive!,* and others; listed in *International Who's Who in Poetry.*

ISABEL MARSHALL, Massachusetts - Widely published in anthologies such as *Dreams, The Poet,* and New Worlds' *Mirrors of the Wistful Dreamer.*

JOHN MASCAZINE, Ohio - Published in several literary magazines; a senior in college, who plans to teach in grammar school.

OLIVIA McCORMACK, Colorado - Her poems "The Wind Flows Free" and "I Ride Against the Wind" will appear next fall in *New Voices in American Poetry.*

JUDITH ANNE McCRARY, California - Secretary of her senior class at Poway High; published in *Teen Magazine*; does volunteer work at Balboa Naval Hospital.

MARK McNEASE, Washington - New Worlds 1981 Poetry Contest winner.

BETTY D. MERCER, Michigan - Published her poetry book: *Toward a Brighter Tomorrow-A First Collection of Twenty-Seven Poems.* She is a certified electrolysis specialist.

CHERYL MICUCCI, New York - High school English teacher; awarded Honorable Mention awards from The American Song Festival and from Writer's Digest.

DAVID MONREAL, California - Has published poems and short stories. "My plans for the future are very simple: To continue to write, and hopefully write better all the time."

KENT MONROE JR., Tennessee - University of Tennessee student; published in *Voices International, College Poetry Review, Mockingbird,* and *Hometowner.*

PAT MORA, Texas - Teaches English at the University of Texas; published in *Amphora Review* and others.

JENNIFER MORRIS, New York - Actress/Singer; member of Wisconsin Fellowship of Poets.

DIANNE J. MORRISSEY, California - Her poetry has been reproduced for calendars, enjoyed over radio network, and illustrated in works by John Hamilton, calligrapher.

VICKI S. MOSSMAN, Colorado - Published in New Worlds' *Mirrors....*, in *Dreams*, and *Honey Creek*. "Jerry, thanks again for your friendship. You are a special part of my life."

BETTY MUSCHAR, Pennsylvania - Has published in *Mirrors...* and various other anthologies.

ALICIA J. MUSE, Kentucky - A junior at Fleming County High; her first formal publication; also enjoys artistic and musical expressions.

ELLEN H. MUSE, Kentucky - Widely published in anthologies; a member of several poetry societies and an award recipient; photographer and composer.

NATALIE A. NALEPINSKI, California - "A 16 year old who believes in hugging and happy faces. It is solely by God's will that she is able to do what she loves best: write poetry."

ALAN NAPIER, Ohio - Recipient of the Engleman Award, for a play, and has been published in *Cedar Rock*, *The Literary Review*, and many others.

NICHOLAS, California - Author of many enjoyable poetry collections.

ROBERT J. OBERG, Rhode Island - Published in *The Poet*, *Anyart Journal*, and New Worlds' *Mirrors of the Wistful Dreamer*.

ELEANOR OTTO, New York - In January, 1981, was awarded a Cultural Doctorate in Literature by the World University in Tucson, Arizona.

DAVID J. PATAROZZI, Illinois - Published in *The Poet*.

JANET PEMBOR, Illinois - An artist; studied creative writing with Roy and Priscilla Cadwell, founders of the Lester B. Pearson Peace Park.

CAROLY POE, Ohio - Published in *Grit*, *Wings*, *Poetry Corner*, *Lyrical Voices*, New Worlds anthologies, and others.

GLORIA H. PROCSAL, California - Her poetry, essays, and short stories have been published in countless literary magazines here and abroad. Author of three poetry collections.

GAIL RAZINSKY, New York - Homemaker, duenna to two prissy cats, and an inveterate writer of verse.

FLOYD M. REGAN, JR., Florida - "Enjoys tropical fish, reading, writing, and Sheila."

BONNIE RIECHERT, Georgia - A science writer currently finishing a master's degree program in journalism - interested in ethics in journalism, public understanding of science, social psychology, and communication law.

BEV FOX ROBERSON, Virginia - Works in accounting while pursuing a college degree; last year won first place in the annual John Tyler College poetry contest, and this year won first and second place awards.

MATTHEW ROGERS, Michigan - Fourteen years old, a student at Pathfinder School in Traverse City, Michigan.

STEVEN B. ROGERS, Maryland - Authored three volumes of German verse; co-authored a play, *Let There Be Light!*; founded and edits Rainfeather Press.

ROSE MARIE ROTH, Michigan - An actress in little theater; a mother of six children; her first publication.

REBECCA S. ROSSIGNOL, Maine - New Worlds 1981 Poetry Contest winner.

LEN ROTONDARO, Connecticut - High school teacher; coaches girls' track and field; published in *Dragonfly*, *The Little Apple*, and others.

DONNA S. RUTSKY, Colorado - Interested in poetry therapy and music.

PAT ST. PIERRE, Connecticut - Besides poems, published five short stories for children in *Look and Listen*, *More*, and *Adventure* magazines.

VIRGIE McCOY SAMMONS, Georgia - Been published for some time: anthologies, magazines...

MARY LOU SANELLI, Washington - Published in *The Archipelago*, *The Stone*, *Creative Review*, and others.

JOHN T. SAVINO, New York - Published in *RAM*, *World of Poetry*, *Poetry Press*, *Fairlane House*, and Young Publications; working on his own poetry collection.

ROBERT J. SAVINO, New York - Recently completed first collection of poems, *The Stranger Inside Me*; also writes children's stories.

JOHN A. SCARFFE, Kansas - Former high school teacher; will now attend Kansas University and work towards a Master's degree in journalism.

MARGARET L. SCHELL, Colorado - "I am 78 years old and have had nearly 500 poems published."

LINDA JEAN SCHUTZ, California - "Have been writing since my first poem was published, at the age of eight. Currently employed in the publishing field. Hope to someday successfully combine photography and writing into a freelance career.

DON SEARS, California - Noted poet, linguist, and scholar; this year's Outstanding Professor Award recipient at Cal. State Fullerton.

GREG SENN, Wisconsin - Recently had work published in *Sweetwater Review*. This is his first appearance in an anthology.

DAWN LANGLEY SIMMONS, New York - Wife of John-Paul Simmons, folk sculptor; daughter of actress Dame Margaret Rutherford, and mother of Natasha Manigault Simmons, 9. Author of biographies.

DAVID T. SMITH, Georgia - Writing poetry since seventh grade; hobbies are archaeology, anthropology, paleoanthropology, and writing poetry.

LEE SMITH, West Virginia - A sophomore at Marshall University, majoring in English and magazine journalism; enjoys music, art, and writing.

RUSTY STANDRIDGE, Arkansas - A creative writing major at Arkansas Tech, where he is learning his craft under the tutelage of B.C. Hall.

ALEXANDRA STOLL, New York - Off-Broadway actress, playwright, poem published in *Encore*.

LINDA LEE STUBBS, New Jersey - Member of NOW and WOW (Women Office Workers); editor of *NOW's News*, monthly newsletter for Passaic County NOW; member of N.J. Poetry Society.

JIM SUTPHIN, Connecticut - A credit analyst. A graduate of Fredonia State University, whose hobby is life.

ALICE MACKENZIE SWAIM, Pennsylvania - New Worlds 1981 Poetry Contest winner.

CHRISTINE SWANBERG, Illinois - Published in *Dramatics Magazine, The English Journal, Lively Times, Esprit*, and others; a former editor of *The Rockford Review*.

ROBERT TAYLOR, Arizona - "36, single, wrote this poem after my marriage ended; I also paint and play the guitar."

JOHN TERLESKY, Pennsylvania - Eighteen years old, assistant at country club; interested in film, writing, and oration.

LINDA BETH TOTH, West Virginia - New Worlds 1981 Poetry Contest winner. Summa cum laude graduate of the University of Virginia; Shakespearean professor; published widely: *English Journal, Showcase, Eternal Echoes*, and others.

STEVE TROYANOVICH, New Jersey - Presently working on a series of translations and critical studies of modern French-Canadian poets, with emphasis upon the work of Fernand Ouellette.

MARY LOUISE TULLOSS, Maryland - 22, full-time secretary in Georgetown; takes evening classes for a paralegal career; interested in acting, politics, classical music, etc.

WARREN W. VACHÉ, New Jersey - A jazz musician (string bass) and jazz writer published in many musical journals; just completed a biography of Pee Wee Erwin, noted jazz musician.

DAVID VAJDA, New Jersey - Published in *The Archer, Exit, Wind, Abbey*, etc.; editor of Ptolemy/The Browns Mills Review Press.

JON VARGA, California - Studied piano in college with several prominent concert artists. Published in *The Poet, Arulo!*, and *Encore*.

RENÉE VIOSCA, Louisiana - Has four university degrees, two of them Ph.D.'s; published all over the world (1,350 poems and 40 prose pieces).

KEITH VLASAK, Ohio - Published in *Poem, Voices International, The Poet, Gusto*, and New Worlds.

E.I.V. von HEITLINGER, Illinois - Mechanical engineer, painter, sculptor, musician. I "do not think of poetry as 'work,' just 'rockets and rainbows.'"

PAVLA VRSIC, Texas - A member of Mensa, recently graduated from high school. Interested in music, medicine, travel, coin and stamp collecting, and more.

M. WAD, Georgia - Member of the Dixie Council of Authors; actor, player, dramatist, freelance writer; published in *Church Educator* and *World of Poetry*.

MELISSA McCLELLAN WARE, Florida - An ornamental horticulturist; for nine years writing has been a major aspect of her life; currently, she is working with photography to further define her poetry.

CLO WEIRICH, Iowa - New Worlds 1981 Poetry Contest winner.

DON L. WHITE, Kansas - Retired teacher and minister, freelance writer, member of The Authors Guild and Authors League of America; widely published.

ELIZABETH WHITBECK, Connecticut - New Worlds 1981 Poetry Contest winner.

IRENE K. WILSON, Massachusetts - Listed in Poets and Writers, New York; her first book of poems, *Wildflowers of the Mind*, was just published.

CYNTHIA WOLFER, California - Published in New Worlds' *Visions...* and *Samisdat*.

JOSEPH WOLLENWEBER, California - "presently living in San Francisco. No birth, no story but the story which occurs when all that I am not is forgotten."

VANESSA WRIGHT, Illinois - A 17 year old college sophomore.

H.K. YEAGER, Missouri - Published in *Eras Review*, *Kingdom Daily News*, and *Kemperite*; a member of New York Poetry Forum.

LAURA YON, California - A talented dancer, high school junior, who hopes to pursue dual careers: dance and sports training with a dance company.

B. WAYNE ZAJAC, New Jersey - "I thank my parents, my teachers for their encouragement and objective appraisal; most of all, I thank God, crediting the endower and refiner of my gift."

INGRIDA ZEBELINS, Florida - An education coordinator of a medical technology school; main interests are poetry and photography, which she hopes to someday combine.

Only those contributors who sent us biographical information are listed above.

MEMBER
COSMEP
COMMITTEE OF SMALL MAGAZINE
EDITORS AND PUBLISHERS
BOX 703 SAN FRANCISCO, CA 94101